ETHICAL ISSUES IN GLOBAL
BUYER-SUPPLIER RELATIONSHIPS

by

Craig R. Carter, Ph.D.
Assistant Professor of International Supply Chain Management
The Robert H. Smith School of Business
University of Maryland

ACKNOWLEDGMENTS •

The Center for Advanced Purchasing Studies and the author would like to thank the companies that contributed to this research by participating in focus group interviews and by completing the survey questionnaire. Special thanks go to the many companies that participated in the study's focus group interviews; these interviews provided the basis for developing the research questions and survey questionnaire.

Several purchasing executives also contributed to the study by helping to formulate the research and by reviewing the manuscript and providing suggestions for improvement. While those who contributed are too numerous to mention here, special thanks go to:

Tim Coats, Vice Presidennt of Strategic Sourcing, The Pillsbury Company
Louis J. Fournier, Director of Materials, The Toro Company
Maxine Kesten, Director of Purchasing, The Dial Corporation
Gary J. Klco, C.P.M., Senior Purchasing Manager, Cargill
Jack Porter, Manager of Central Purchasing, Caterpillar, Inc.
David Sorensen, Vice President of Purchasing, General Mills, Inc.
Michael Upton, Director of Materials, Phelps Dodge Corporation
Tom Wood, Vice President of Purchasing and Logistics, The Valspar Corporation

Finally, I would like to thank the members of the CAPS staff who contributed to the completion of this study: Kerri Christiansen and Maureen Graff for their administrative assistance with the focus group interviews and survey questionnaire; Richard A. Boyle, Ph.D., Assistant Director and Carol L. Ketchum, Assistant Director at CAPS, for carefully editing the manuscript and helping with the numerous administrative details that made the study possible; and Phillip L. Carter, D.B.A., Director of CAPS for his encouragement, guidance, and support.

Of course, complete responsibility for the final study rests with the author of this report.

ISBN: 0-945968-32-9

CONTENTS •

FIGURES, TABLES, AND APPENDICES •

EXECUTIVE SUMMARY •

INTRODUCTION

From Watergate through Irangate to Whitewater in government, and from Lopez at Volkswagen to ADM in private industry, the presence of unethical behavior appears to be a perennial topic of media coverage. Ethical and socially responsible behavior can positively affect a firm's image and reputation. For example, Ben and Jerry's prominent contributions to social causes have helped the former start-up company's annual sales grow to more than $150 million.

On the other hand, there are costs associated with unethical activity, including fines, liability, and negative publicity. Consider the following quotes, which recently appeared on the front page of the *Wall Street Journal* in a single day (August 6, 1997, pp. A1):

> "Igene filed suit against ADM, alleging the big grain processor stole secrets regarding the biotech firm's process for producing a pigment to turn farm-raised salmon pink."

> "Columbia/HCA faces a separate investigation by Florida officials to determine whether the firm committed Medicaid fraud, state officials said."

> "Picking through a fat legal bill, auditors for the Citadel found something that really bugged their client ... the Citadel's nemesis, the American Civil Liberties Union, had included the $524 cost of a going-away party for an ACLU staffer who had worked on the high-profile case against the military academy."

Purchasing managers in particular can have significant influence over a firm's reputation. Because these individuals interact frequently with suppliers and other upstream channel members, their behavior can and does affect how the firm is viewed by suppliers and other outside organizations.

The purchasing function controls more than 60 percent of a firm's sales dollars in some industries; considerable temptation toward unethical behavior can exist when such large amounts of money are involved. Further, like marketing and sales, purchasing is a boundary-spanning function that, because of its interaction with other members of the supply chain and its exposure to a firm's external environment, may be under considerable pressure to depart from accepted norms of behavior and ethical standards set by the firm. Past research has shown that those parts of an organization that are most exposed to the outside environment are in turn most

likely to deviate from the firm's behavioral standards, including those behaviors related to ethics.

DEFINING ETHICS

Because a list of possible ethical actions would be much longer than a list of possible unethical activities, the issue of ethics is usually discussed within the context of unethical actions and behaviors. For this reason, the author concentrates on unethical activities in buyer-supplier relationships. For the purpose of this study, unethical activities are defined as ***the specific set of actions taken within the buyer-supplier relationship that are considered unacceptable, inappropriate, or irresponsible by purchasing managers and their suppliers.***

While these issues have been examined in the past within a domestic context, there has been relatively little research concerning ethical issues surrounding the relationships of American buyers and their foreign suppliers. For example, do American buyers view ethical activities differently from their foreign suppliers? If so, are there further differences among the perceptions of European, Latin American, and Asian suppliers? A combination of focus group interviews and mail surveys of U.S. purchasing managers and their foreign suppliers were used to identify the specific unethical actions in these buyer-supplier relationships. These issues and others are expanded upon next through the introduction of the study's broad research objectives and more narrowly focused research questions.

OBJECTIVES OF THE RESEARCH

The researcher is not suggesting that purchasing managers are inherently unethical. Further, the author is not going to comment on the overall level of reported activities in terms of whether those activities should be judged as ethical or unethical. Rather, the purpose of the study is to examine:

1. what factors impact the level of unethical activities

2. whether differences exist between the perceptions of buyers and their supplier counterparts in terms of unethical activities involved in global buyer-supplier relationships

3. the impact the level of unethical activities has on such outcomes as satisfaction with and effectiveness of the buyer-supplier relationship

To address these broad objectives, seven specific research questions were formulated. A combination of focus group interviews and survey results from purchasing managers and their foreign suppliers were used to answer the study's research questions. This executive summary provides an abbreviated overview of the answers to these research questions. However, because ethics is a less tangible subject than other purchasing-related issues and includes both overt as well as more subtle unethical activities and behaviors, it is strongly recommended that the reader review the detailed discussion of the results appearing in the main body of this report to better understand the relationships and insights highlighted in this summary.

RESEARCH QUESTIONS

Research Question 1: What are the specific activities that encompass ethical issues in global buyer-supplier relationships?

Unethical activities surrounding global buyer-supplier relationships discussed in this report were identified through a combination of group interviews with purchasing managers, a mail questionnaire, and a review of the relevant ethics literature.

Unethical Practices Identified through the Focus Group Interviews

The focus group interviewees unanimously agreed that lying to a supplier was explicitly unethical. The focus group discussions also complimented the findings from the literature review, which suggested that there are a number of less tangible ways in which deception can occur. These activities include using ambiguous contract terms or other forms of communication to gain an advantage over the other party, exaggerating the seriousness of a problem to gain concessions, overestimating demand to gain volume discounts, overcommiting resources or production schedules, or in any similar way misleading the other party.

Interviewees also unanimously agreed that breaking the law was unethical. From an international standpoint, the Foreign Corrupt Practices Act and the Omnibus Trade Act of 1988 regulate conditions under which payment may be made to foreign officials. The Acts make it illegal for American companies and their employees to make payments or give gifts of significant value to foreign officials. Bribery of a foreign official regarding a critical decision, such as allowing a firm to obtain or retain business, is illegal. However, other types of bribery, such as facilitating payments, are however, legal. Facilitating payments are bribes to lower level officials that create an incentive to more promptly perform routine activities that would have been performed as part of their duties regardless of whether the payment was made. Examples of these routine activities include loading or unloading cargo, processing goods through customs, and processing other paperwork related to international trade.

Ethical actions mean more than just obeying the law or avoiding deceit. There are many other activities that, while not involving outright deception, were also considered by focus group participants to be potentially unethical. These activities included allowing personalities and friendships to influence decisions, accepting a bid or allowing a favored supplier to rebid after the closing date, canceling purchase orders in progress and trying to avoid cancellation charges, and asking the other party for proprietary information about competitors. Examples of proprietary information include price and cost data, proprietary knowledge concerning software and production processes, and suppliers' bids. Other unethical activities related to the competitive bidding process include writing specifications that favor a particular supplier, and soliciting quotations from suppliers who have no or little chance of success.

Specific supplier activities that were identified as being unethical included increasing prices when there is a shortage of supply and knowingly overcommitting resources or production schedules. Other supplier activities that the focus group participants suggested may be unethical include using less competitive prices or terms for buyers who purchase exclusively from the supplier, and avoiding personnel in purchasing by approaching personnel in such departments as engineering or manufacturing. Bribery and the offering of gifts in excess of nominal value were identified as unethical activities that were perhaps more applicable on an international scale.

Survey Results

A survey of American purchasing managers and their foreign suppliers was used to further narrow the scope of these activities and behaviors as well as to generalize these findings and examine the factors that affect and are influenced by unethical activities in the buyer-supplier relationship. An analysis of the survey data from buying firms indicated that unethical activities of buyers fall into two broad categories:

a) *Deceitful Practices:* This first category consisted of behaviors involving deception, and included survey questions addressing the following activities:

   • Purposefully misleading a salesperson in a negotiation
   • Exaggerating the seriousness of a problem to gain concessions
   • Using obscure contract terms to gain an advantage over suppliers
   • Inventing (making up) a second source of supply to gain competitive advantage.

b) *Subtle Practices:* The second category of unethical actions included somewhat more subtle activities such as:

   • Writing specifications that favor a particular supplier
   • Allowing personalities of suppliers to impact decisions
   • Giving preference to suppliers preferred by top management.

A further analysis of the survey data from buying firms suggested that unethical activities of *suppliers* consisted of a single set of activities, including:

- Knowingly overcommitting resources or production schedules
- Lying or grossly misleading customers in a negotiation
- Using obscure contract terms to gain an advantage over suppliers
- Asking for information about competitors
- Offering gifts in excess of nominal value
- Increasing prices when there is a shortage
- Using backdoor selling techniques such as approaching personnel is engineering, manufacturing, or other departments outside of purchasing
- Using less competitive terms or prices for buyers who purchase exclusively from the supplier.

Finally, it is interesting to note that an analysis of the supplier survey data revealed that suppliers identified the same sets of unethical activities (for both buyers and suppliers) as did buyers.

Research Question 2: Are there differences between the perceptions of buyers and suppliers regarding the level of unethical behavior in the relationships?

The survey data revealed significant differences between the perceptions of buyers and their suppliers regarding deceitful and subtle practices of buyers and supplier activities. One explanation may be that buyers are not accurately communicating their intentions to their suppliers. For example, suppliers may believe that a buyer is exaggerating the seriousness of a problem to gain price concessions or improve service levels, while the buyer believes the problem legitimately exists. Similarly, the buyer may actually be considering a second source of supply, unbeknownst to the supplier.

Conversely, some foreign suppliers might offer gifts in excess of nominal value because this reflects their culture and customs. Buyers in some American companies accept these gifts because they realize the suppliers are giving these gifts as a sign of respect, rather than seeking to gain influence. Further comments by purchasing managers suggested, however, that the gifts were almost always donated or in some other fashion given to the purchasing firm, rather than the individual buyer. As a result, buyers may not consider this to be a gift in excess of nominal value because they do not personally receive the gift.

Research Question 3: What are the organizational factors that affect the ethicality of global buyer-supplier relationships?

A number of organizational factors were identified through the focus group interviews that might affect buyers' involvement in unethical activities. These factors include the actions of management and co-workers, the inclusion of ethical issues in formal evaluations, training in ethics, and ethics policies. The survey data suggested:

a. The key organizational factors influencing buyers' involvement in deceitful practices are:
   - Communicating ethics policies to suppliers
   - Having an ethics hotline in place

b. Subtle practices are affected most by the following organizational factors:
   - Including ethical issues in formal evaluations
   - Providing training regarding ethical issues

These results suggest that some employees might engage in deceitful practices regardless of such factors as training or leadership by example. Instead, the only viable deterrent may be the fear of getting caught or reported, which would be more likely to occur when policies are communicated to suppliers and when firms have an ethics hotline in place.

Whereas engaging in deceitful practices can be perceived as more clearly unethical, the activities that encompass subtle practices fall into more of a gray area. Training appears to help educate buyers and make them aware of these more subtle ethical issues. This may not only be useful for new and inexperienced purchasing managers, but also for more seasoned personnel who find themselves in unfamiliar situations. Similarly, including ethical issues in a buyer's formal evaluations can help to reinforce material and policies covered during training.

Research Question 4: How do a buyer's and supplier's pressure to perform affect the ethicality of global buyer-supplier relationships?

With the increase in downsizing and leaner organizations, clearly employees feel increased pressure to perform well in their positions. Interestingly, there were no significant differences in the level of deceitful or subtle practices among buyers who experienced high versus low pressure to perform in their positions. The researcher found similar results with the foreign suppliers.

One possible explanation for these findings is that savvy buyers realize that if they're engaged in unethical practices, they will only hurt themselves professionally in the long-run. First, their company's reputation will be damaged. If an agreement is entered into unethically, or if unethical actions occur during the course of a contract, this is not a win-win transaction or even a win-lose deal. This becomes a lose-lose situation. When the contract opens up again, the supplier may choose not to do business with the buying firm. Further, as suggested by one of the study's participants, "pretty soon word gets out and everyone is adding 10 percent into their pricing because of the buying company's unethical reputation. It's the cost of doing business, and suppliers figure that out."

Many buyers probably also realize that unethical behavior will hurt them personally. It's likely that buyers who act unethically towards suppliers will not only lose the trust of those suppliers, but also of those people inside the buying firm with whom they deal. Similarly, if a salesperson acts unethically, he will probably lose the trust of, and consequently the business from, the buyer. Participants indicated that it's a "small world" and that an unethical reputation can spread quickly, not only within a company but throughout companies in an industry.

Research Question 5: What external factors affect the ethicality of global buyer-supplier relationships?

This research question examined the following issues:

- Is it possible that as the duration of a buying firm's relationship with a supplier increases, the presence of unethical behavior decreases?
- How does the nature of a purchasing manager's relationship with their international suppliers influence unethical activities?
- Does the foreign supplier's nationality play any part in unethical actions of either buyers or suppliers?

An analysis of the survey data found no relationship between unethical practices and the length of time the buyer-supplier relationship had been in existence, nor between the type of relationship that buyers had with their foreign suppliers and unethical activities. It appears that buyers and suppliers will engage in unethical practices (whether to a great extent, not at all, or somewhere in between) regardless of these factors.

A supplier's nationality was also unrelated to the level of unethical activities found in the buyer-supplier relationship. The realm of behaviors and activities considered unethical by American purchasing managers appear to be well communicated and understood by their international suppliers. The surveyed suppliers have most likely gained this understanding not only through their current relationships with the surveyed buyers, but also through prior relationships with other American buying firms. While differences in ethical values do almost certainly still exist when transactions occur *within* some foreign countries, this too may change as even local business continues to become increasingly international in character.

Research Question 6: How does the level of unethical activity affect satisfaction with the global buyer-supplier relationship?

As anticipated, a significant, negative relationship was found between a supplier's level of unethical activities and a buyer's satisfaction with the supplier relationship. As the unethical activities of a supplier increased, the buyer's satisfaction decreased. While unethical activities on the part of suppliers may result in short-term gains, buyers become dissatisfied. This dissatisfaction may ultimately lead to decreased sales or even termination of the relationship by a buying firm.

The researcher also calculated difference or "gap" scores between buyers' and suppliers' perceptions of deceitful practices, subtle practices, and supplier activities. An analysis of the survey data suggests that when large gaps between buyers' and suppliers' perceptions regarding deceitful practices of buyers exist, buyers are

less satisfied with the relationship. This corresponds to earlier input from study participants who indicated that while those engaged in deceitful practices may achieve short-term gains, they will be less satisfied with the relationship in the long run, as suppliers refuse to renew contracts and continue with the relationship.

Research Question 7: How does the level of unethical activity affect the effectiveness of the global buyer-supplier relationship?

The researcher also found that as the unethical actions of a supplier increase, buyers begin to believe that suppliers are performing less effectively. As one participant suggested, "You kind of wonder what they are hiding, now that they have to resort to this type of activity in order to stay on as a supplier or become a supplier." Similarly, a participant related an account of a salesperson who lied to a buyer's manager to hide production problems at the supplier's plant. This not only resulted in lowering the buying firm's satisfaction, but also reduced their perception of the supplier's performance in terms of service, quality, and price.

SUMMARY AND IMPLICATIONS

The findings of this research point to a number of factors that can affect the level of purchasing's involvement in unethical activities. Unethical behavior in the buyer-supplier relationship can negatively affect the satisfaction of both buyers and suppliers, and even the buyer's perception of how effectively a supplier performs; however, this is not true of all types of unethical activity. Finally, the activities viewed as being unethical are consistent across national cultures, at least when foreign suppliers are dealing with American buyers. These findings are summarized below:

1. Foreign suppliers identified as unethical the same categories of activities as did U.S. buyers. One possible explanation for this is that these buyers and suppliers judge the identified activities similarly because they involve fundamental, core values that cross cultures. Perhaps a more realistic explanation for this similarity between buyers' and suppliers' perceptions is that ethical expectations and standards have been established and communicated as part of the buyer-supplier relationship, as well as through an international supplier's affiliations with other American companies.

2. The ethical issues involved in the relationships between American buyers and their foreign suppliers appear to be the same as those found in domestic sourcing. For example, analysis of the survey data found that activities such as bribery and the use of "grease (facilitating) payments," which have typically been associated with international transactions,

were not included in either of the two buyer categories of unethical practices or unethical supplier activities. This suggests that U.S. buyers are not engaging in these activities nearly as often as might have been the case in the past. Further, international suppliers appear to realize that these activities are unacceptable when dealing with American buyers.

3. While the surveyed buyers and suppliers identified the same dimensions of unethical actions, significant differences did exist between buyers' and suppliers' perceptions regarding how involved each believed the other to be in these activities. It is important to realize that even the *appearance* of an unethical action can affect a party's perception of how ethical the other party's behavior really is. For example, a supplier may be confident that it can meet a promised production schedule but then experience production delays and be unable to deliver as promised. While the supplier may not believe that it has acted in an unethical manner, the buyer may perceive that the supplier has knowingly, and thus unethically, over-committed resources or production schedules. It is therefore important for both buyers and suppliers to openly communicate their intentions and all relevant details of the purchasing transaction, in order to minimize the "gaps" that can occur between each party's perception of the other's behavior.

4. The deceitful practices of buyers are minimized when companies communicate ethics policies to suppliers and have an ethics hotline in place. Other organizational factors, such as top management's "walking the talk" or providing training *appear to have no impact on the degree to which purchasing managers are involved in this dimension of unethical buyer activities.* Thus, the only practical deterrent appears to be the fear of getting caught or reported, which would be more likely to occur when policies are communicated to suppliers and when firms have an ethics hotline in place.

5. The less obviously unethical activities comprising buyer's subtle practices were affected by both ethics training and the inclusion of ethical issues in an employee's formal evaluation. Ethics training can help make new, inexperienced, and even seasoned buyers more aware of these less obvious, unethical behaviors. In turn, including ethical issues as a part of a buyer's formal evaluations can help to reinforce material and policies covered during training.

6. It is easy to assume that buyers who are under pressure to perform and who want to advance in their careers may be more likely to engage in unethical practices. This is not the case. Similarly, there is no relationship between pressures felt by foreign supplier representatives and their involvement in unethical activities. It appears that both buyers and suppliers realize that employing unethical practices will result in short-term success at best, but will inevitably culminate in damage to both their careers and the buyer-supplier relationship.

7. The researcher found no relationship between the supplier's nationality and the level of unethical activity in the buyer-supplier relationship. One explanation for this finding is that the behaviors and activities considered unethical by American purchasing managers have been well communicated to and are understood to be unethical by their foreign suppliers. Norms and expectations regarding ethics may have also been established through the foreign supplier's prior relationships with other U.S. buying firms. It is important to note that these findings apply only to U.S. buyers and their foreign suppliers. Interviews with purchasing managers suggest that different scenarios may exist when purchasing occurs outside of the United States for a foreign-based plant or subsidiary.

8. The author also found no link between unethical practices and either the length or type of relationship that exists between the buyer and supplier. Once norms and behaviors are established in a relationship, it is unlikely that time alone will change those practices. Similarly, the nature of the buyer's relationship with their suppliers is not related to the level of unethical behavior found in those relationships. Apparently, if purchasing managers or suppliers decide to act unethically, they will do so regardless of the type of relationship they have established with the other firm. As one informant suggested, "The old phrase 'he'd cheat his own mother,' has a certain amount of truth. Whether it's a partner or a seller, if you are going to be unethical, the identity of the party getting short shrift makes little difference." Conversely, firms that choose to conduct business in an ethical manner will do so regardless of whether the relationship consists of a one-time transaction, a long-term contract, or a strategic alliance.

9. Buyers who were least satisfied with the supplier relationship were those who perceived their suppliers to be the most involved in unethical practices. Buyers were also the least satisfied if their own organizations were involved in deceitful practices. While deception may allow buyers to achieve short-term gains, they will be less satisfied with the relationship in the long-run, as suppliers increase prices or refuse to renew contracts.

10. When buyers perceive that suppliers are involved in unethical practices, they also believe that suppliers are performing less effectively. Buyers begin to wonder whether suppliers are trying to mask problems with production or quality, and believe that the supplier's performance is reduced in terms of service and price.

DESIGN OF THE STUDY •

OBJECTIVES

This study was conducted to answer the following research questions:

1. What are the specific activities that encompass ethical issues in global buyer-supplier relationships?

2. Are there differences between the perceptions of buyers and their suppliers regarding the level of unethical behavior in the relationship?

3. What are the organizational factors that affect the ethicality of global buyer-supplier relationships?

4. How do a buyer's and supplier's pressure to perform affect the ethicality of global buyer-supplier relationships?

5. What external factors affect the ethicality of global buyer-supplier relationships?

6. How does the level of unethical activity affect satisfaction with the global buyer-supplier relationship?

7. How does the level of unethical activity affect the effectiveness of the global buyer-supplier relationship?

DESIGN

The study consists of two primary segments: (1) a series of focus group and individual interviews; and (2) a set of survey questionnaires sent to American purchasing managers and their international suppliers.

Focus Group Interviews

The purpose of conducting these types of interviews was to build upon the findings of a literature review of ethics research by further determining the range of possible activities that might comprise ethical activities in international buyer-supplier relationships. Focus group interviews in particular were chosen so that attention could be shifted away from the interviewer toward the participants, with the goal of encouraging a brainstorming of ideas by participants. It is important to note however, that the focus group interviews were also conducted as a carefully planned discussion that followed a structured questioning route (see Appendix A).

The focus group interviews were conducted with purchasing managers from companies that purchase from international suppliers. These firms represent a diverse group of industries, including consumer products, aerospace, pharmaceuticals, construction equipment, and foodstuffs.

Survey Questionnaire Segment

Based on the findings from the interviews and from an examination of existing literature in the area of ethics, a survey questionnaire was generated and pretested. The final buyers' questionnaire and the matched, nearly identical suppliers' questionnaire used for the study are shown in Appendices B and C. This second nearly identical questionnaire was sent to suppliers of the surveyed buyers, allowing the researcher to examine not only the perspectives of purchasing managers but also the matched perspectives of their suppliers.

The Sample

The survey was sent to the purchasing organizations of 1,300 U.S. firms. This sample consisted of members of the National Association of Purchasing Management (NAPM), participants in previous CAPS purchasing performance benchmarking studies, and participants in the 1997 CAPS-sponsored Executive Purchasing Roundtable. Respondents from the buying firms were asked to focus most of their responses on their relationship with a particular supplier, and were also asked to forward the second questionnaire to the chosen international supplier. Like the buyer survey, this supplier questionnaire was returned directly to CAPS. The supplier was also asked to specifically consider the buyer's firm when answering the survey questions.

A total of 132 surveys were received from the buying firms and 88 surveys were received from suppliers. Another 157 surveys were returned stating that the survey subject was not applicable because the buying firms did not purchase from international suppliers. This resulted in an 11.5 percent response rate from buyers and a 66.7 percent response rate from their suppliers. In addition, follow-up phone calls to nonrespondents indicated that the primary reason for not participating in the survey was its nonapplicability, because the buying firm purchased only domestically. As a result, the actual response rate for eligible firms is most likely quite a bit higher than reported here.

While the 88 matched buyer-supplier surveys may seem small, this number is actually higher than average for this type of research method, where matched responses are solicited across organizations using a set of mail surveys. For example, over a five-year period in the *Journal of Marketing,* the average number of matched buyer-supplier surveys reported for this type of methodology was 51. In addition, a similar survey method used by Hendrick and Ellram (1993) generated 98 matched pairs of surveys from buyers and their suppliers.

Nonresponse Bias

Despite the results of past studies, the response rate from buyers was still quite low. An attempt was made to determine whether nonresponse bias exists. Nonresponse bias occurs when the opinions and perceptions of the survey respondents do not accurately represent the overall sample to whom the survey was sent. One test for nonresponse bias is to compare the answers of early versus late respondents to the survey (Lambert & Harrington, 1990). The theory is that late respondents are more likely to answer the questionnaire like nonrespondents than are early respondents (Armstrong & Overton, 1977).

A multivariate T test was computed using the key study variables in order to determine whether significant differences existed between early and late respondents. The results suggest that early respondents do not display statistically significant differences from late respondents ($p = 0.3613$).

Social Desirability Bias

Social desirability bias occurs in survey research when respondents inaccurately answer questions to conform to social norms or the expectations of the researcher, in order to portray themselves in a more favorable light. In order to solicit candid responses about their level of involvement in unethical activities, purchasing personnel were asked to answer these questions in terms of the activities of the purchasing department in general, rather than the actions of the individual buyer or purchasing manager. A similar technique was used by Rudelius and Buchholz (1979) in an attempt to minimize social desirability bias. Further, it has been shown that this type of "other-based" questioning is more effective in lowering social desirability bias than the most commonly used alternate method, the randomized response technique (Armacost et al., 1991).

In addition to taking this precautionary measure, a scale was included in the survey to measure social desirability bias. This scale was an abbreviated version of the Crowne-Marlowe Social Desirability Scale (Crowne & Marlowe, 1960). The scale used in the survey was shorted due to length considerations and the nonapplicability of some of the scale items in the original Crowne-Marlowe Social Desirability Scale, which was developed for the population in general rather than a specific business-related population.

The mean of the four totaled scale items was 0.96, with a score of zero representing no social desirability and 4 representing the presence of social desirability bias. The relatively low mean score suggests that respondents answered the survey questions without distorting their responses to appear as though their firms are less involved in unethical activities than they actually are.

Statistical Methods Used and Glossary of Terms

p: Throughout this report, the investigator will report a "p," or probability, value. For example, the researcher may report "$p<0.0001$," or "$p<0.05$," (p IS LESS THAN 0.0001; p IS LESS THAN 0.05). The researcher may state that the difference between the response of buyers and their suppliers for a particular activity is "significant at $p<0.0001$." This p-value of 0.0001 means that there is only one chance in 10,000 that the difference in responses occurred by chance. Because there is only a slight chance that the difference occurred by coincidence, one would say that there is a "statistically significant difference." For this study, a significant difference in means or a significant relation between two variables was said to exist if a p-value was less than or equal to 0.05.

Regression Analysis and Analysis of Variance: The investigator used these methods to determine which variables, if any (such as training, pressure to perform, the length of time the relationship had been established with the supplier), had a strong influence on the respondents' reported involvement in unethical activities. Regression analysis was also used to determine which dimensions or types of unethical activity were in turn related to such outcomes as the effectiveness of the buyer-supplier relationship and purchasing's satisfaction with the buyer-supplier relationship. The term "negative correlation" suggests that, for example, a high level of training or the existence of a code of ethics will be associated with relatively low levels of unethical behavior in buyer-supplier relationships. Alternatively a "positive correlation" would exist if, for example, higher pressure to perform is related to high levels of unethical behavior in the buyer-supplier relationship.

In multiple regression analysis and ANOVA the researcher hypothesized that the magnitude of one variable, called a "dependent variable" (unethical purchasing activities, for example), is dependent on the degree to which the other variables, called "independent variables" (such as training, leadership by example), are used or exist. Thus, the investigator hypothesized that one or more of a group of independent variables may cause the one dependent variable to be high or low.

A **construct** is a concept or variable, such as *unethical purchasing practices* or *satisfaction with the buyer-supplier relationship*. It would have been difficult to assess some of the study's constructs using a single survey question. For example, it would have been difficult if not impossible to obtain an accurate response to a single question that asked purchasing managers whether their firm was involved in unethical purchasing practices, or how effectively their international suppliers were performing. For this reason, multiple questions were used to measure many of the study's constructs.

Reliability refers to the extent to which scores of survey questions are consistently measuring the same underlying construct. **Validity** refers to the extent to which scale items are actually measuring the construct in question, rather than an alternative construct. The statistical analyses and methodologies used to examine the reliability and validity of the study's constructs are presented and explained in detail in Appendix D.

STUDY RESULTS

After a brief introduction, the next section of the report will present the results from the focus group interviews. These results lead to a definition of ethical issues in buyer-supplier relationships, and to the generation of a number of proposed unethical behaviors and activities that might occur in global buyer-supplier relationships. These behaviors and activities were then incorporated into the survey questionnaire. The results from the survey questionnaires are presented in the order of the study's seven research questions. A summary and conclusions based on these results appear later in the report.

ETHICAL ISSUES IN GLOBAL BUYER-SUPPLIER RELATIONSHIPS •

INTRODUCTION

From Watergate through Irangate to Whitewater in government, and from Lopez at Volkswagen to ADM in private industry, the presence of unethical behavior appears to be a perennial topic of media coverage. Ethical and socially responsible behavior can positively affect a firm's image and reputation. For example, Ben and Jerry's celebrated contributions to social causes have helped the former start-up company's annual sales grow to more than $150 million.

On the other hand, there are costs associated with unethical activity, including fines, liability, and negative publicity. Consider the following quotes, which recently appeared on the front page of the *Wall Street Journal* in a single day (August 6, 1997, pp. A1):

"Igene filed suit against ADM, alleging the big grain processor stole secrets regarding the biotech firm's process for producing a pigment to turn farm-raised salmon pink."

"Columbia/HCA faces a separate investigation by Florida officials to determine whether the firm committed Medicaid fraud, state officials said."

"Picking through a fat legal bill, auditors for the Citadel found something that really bugged their client ... the Citadel's nemesis, the American Civil Liberties Union, had included the $524 cost of a going-away party for an ACLU staffer who had worked on the high-profile case against the military academy."

Purchasing managers in particular can have significant influence over a firm's reputation. Because these individuals interact frequently with suppliers and other upstream channel members, their behavior can and does affect how the firm is viewed by suppliers and other outside organizations (Dobler & Burt, 1996).

The purchasing function controls more than 60 percent of a firm's sales dollars in some industries; considerable temptation toward unethical behavior can exist when such large amounts of money are involved (Leenders & Fearon, 1993). Further, like marketing and sales, purchasing is a boundary-spanning function (Webster, 1992; Williams, Guinipero, & Henthorne, 1994) that, because of its interaction with other members of the supply chain and its exposure to a firm's external environment, may be under considerable pressure to depart from accepted norms of behavior and ethical standards set by the firm (Ferrell & Gresham, 1985). Past research has shown that those parts of an organization that are most exposed to the outside environment are in turn most likely to deviate from the firm's behavioral standards, including those behaviors related to ethics (Osborn & Hunt, 1974).

RESEARCH QUESTIONS

The researcher is not suggesting that purchasing managers are necessarily unethical. Further, the author is not going to comment on the overall level of reported activities in terms of whether those activities should be judged as ethical or unethical. Rather, the purpose of the study is to examine:

1. what factors influence the level of unethical activities

2. whether differences exist between the perceptions of buyers and their supplier counterparts in terms of unethical activities involved in global buyer-supplier relationships

3. the effect that the level of unethical activities has on such outcomes as satisfaction with and effectiveness of the buyer-supplier relationship.

A series of research questions that address these three broad objectives follows.

Research Question 1: What are the specific activities that encompass ethical issues in global buyer-supplier relationships?

NAPM offers a series of ethical guidelines based upon multiple categories of activities that comprise many ethical issues involved in purchasing. However, it is possible that additional activities encompassed within the domain of ethical purchasing are not included in the NAPM guidelines. For example, do purchasing managers perceive social responsibility concerns such as buying from minority-owned businesses and "green" suppliers as falling within the realm of ethical issues?

14

A broad review of the relevant ethics literature, focus group interviews with purchasing managers, and a matched set of mail questionnaires of U.S. purchasing managers and their foreign suppliers were used to identify all relevant ethical issues in global buyer-supplier relationships, including those contained in the NAPM guidelines.

Ethical issues and concern can also change over time (Wood, 1991; Trevisan, 1986). Even in the United States as recently as 35 years ago, the practice of racism and segregation was considered ethical by some and was permitted by law. Within the purchasing context, so-called "sharp practices" such as obtaining bids from unqualified suppliers in order to increase competition were considered perfectly acceptable in the not-so-distant past.

Finally, are the ethical issues involved in international purchasing and relationships with international suppliers different from domestic sourcing, or are the differences between global and domestic purchasing only a matter of degree, as suggested by Dobler and Burt (1996)?

Research Question 2: Are there differences between the perceptions of buyers and suppliers regarding the level of unethical behavior in the relationships?

Are there significant differences between how ethical buyers perceive their own actions to be and how their suppliers view the buyers? Conversely, are there significant differences in how suppliers view themselves and how ethical buyers believe their suppliers to be? If significant differences in perceptions do exist, this might affect the satisfaction with and effectiveness of the buyer-supplier relationship, issues that are addressed in research questions 6 and 7.

Research Question 3: What are the organizational factors that affect the ethicality of global buyer-supplier relationships?

Management literature has investigated ethical issues from a broad perspective of the overall firm, as well as from the perspective of purchasing in particular. A number of organizational factors might affect the ethics of actions of purchasing managers in their dealings with international suppliers.

Acting as role models, in which top purchasing and company managers "walk the talk," is purported to influence the ethical behavior of employees (Dubinsky & Gwin, 1981). Many consider the role of top management to be the key driver of ethical decision making, in terms of providing commitment, leadership, and examples, and in terms of reducing ethical conflicts encountered by employees (Hunt, Chonko, & Wilcox, 1984; Chonko & Hunt, 1985; Chonko, Tanner, & Weeks, 1996). Similarly, the actions of co-workers, both in purchasing and other functions such as sales and marketing, might affect the actions and ethical decision-making processes of purchasing personnel.

Authors have speculated that ethics training programs and seminars might positively influence ethical behavior and activities (Ferrell & Gresham, 1985). While most managers would agree that breaking the law is an unethical activity, other activities, such as showing favoritism towards certain suppliers, are more ambiguous. It is in these gray areas that guidance in the form of ethics training might be particularly helpful.

Turner et al. (1994) found a significant statistical relationship between one particular aspect of unethical purchasing activity, gratuity acceptance, and the existence of a written ethics code or policy. Codes of ethics can serve to effectively communicate the importance of a policy, provide justification for purchasers to act the way they do, and identify penalties for unethical behavior (Rudelius & Buchholz, 1979). Still, evidence of the actual positive effect of such codes is at best mixed, even though they are used widely by organizations (Mathews, 1987; Murphy, 1989).

In addition to codes of ethics, post-purchase audits might influence unethical behavior and activities (Dobler & Burt, 1996). For example, Reebok uses a three-tiered auditing system performed by plant managers, an internal audit team, and an external audit team that makes sure that facilities are run in accordance with local laws as well as Reebok's own standards.

Beets and Killough (1990) note that behavioral standards such as a code of ethics without associated sanctions and evaluation mechanisms are really just window dressing. Appropriate rewards and punishments might not only positively affect the behavior of purchasing personnel, but also serve to demonstrate to those outside of purchasing, including suppliers, the behaviors that the firm really values (Trevino, 1992). Mitchell et al. (1996) found that a reinforcement system including both rewards and sanctions helped to reduce some aspects of illegal activity within a firm. Similarly, instituting an ethics hotline and effectively communicating ethics policies to suppliers may act as deterrents to purchasing personnel tempted to act in an unethical manner.

Research Question 4: How do a buyer's and supplier's pressure to perform affect the ethicality of global buyer-supplier relationships?

The focus group interviews suggested that as firms continue to downsize and cut costs, purchasing personnel are under constant pressure to improve their results. One interview participant stated, "As companies are pushing for improved performance, people will take greater risks and push the envelope ... the fear of losing your job is great." This fourth research question examines whether there are higher levels of unethical purchasing activity among firms in which there is a great deal of pressure to perform, or where purchasing managers as individuals feel significant pressure to perform.

Purchasing personnel who feel a strong pressure to perform might consider certain behaviors as being less unethical than those in firms with less pressure to perform. For example, purchasing managers experiencing high pressure to perform may be more likely to engage in unethical practices, such as using obscure contract terms or exaggerating the seriousness of a problem when doing business with a supplier, in order to achieve price concessions and meet performance goals and expectations.

Research Question 5: What external factors affect the ethicality of global buyer-supplier relationships?

Several prior studies of international and domestic industrial relationships in countries such as Sweden, West Germany, and Great Britain suggest that the length of these relationships could be related to a number of positive outcomes. While not explicitly stated, the length of the buyer-supplier relationship might also decrease the degree of unethical practices that exist between buyers and their suppliers. In particular, a lengthy relationship between buyers and suppliers might be associated with reduced unethical activity as well as a smaller difference or gap between the perceptions of buyers and suppliers. A smaller gap in perceptions may exist because the perceptions of buyers and suppliers might be shaped and formed through a series of iterative interactions (Epstein, 1989).

The type of relationship that purchasing managers have with their international suppliers might also influence the degree of unethical practices found in the relationship. For example, buyer-supplier partnerships and strategic alliances, which are characterized by a long-term perspective of the relationship and a relatively open sharing of information, might also be associated with lower levels of unethical behavior (Ellram & Cooper, 1990; Gardner & Cooper, 1988).

Finally, researchers have shown that differences in work-related values, including ethics, exist across national cultures (Becker & Fritzsche, 1987; Ferrell & Gresham, 1985; Hofstede, 1980; Hunt & Vitell, 1986). This phenomenon might result because individuals who are raised in different countries are exposed to unique cultures, religious beliefs, and values (England, 1975). Others argue that even though there may be different approaches to dealing with ethical issues, this does not necessarily mean that there are "country differences in ethical principles, nor that it is impossible to formulate universal ethical principles," (Schlegelmilch & Robertson, 1995, pp. 874).

Even in cases in which individuals from different countries agree that an activity is unethical, the degree to which they consider the activity to be unethical can vary. For example, Russians view black market activity to be inevitable in an economy with chronic shortages, and thus view this activity as being less unethical than American managers do (Puffer & McCarthy, 1995). Thus, the nationality of the supplier could influence the level of unethical activities within the relationship, as well as the potential gap that may exist between buyers' and suppliers' perceptions regarding that activity.

Research Question 6: How does the level of unethical activity affect satisfaction with the global buyer-supplier relationship?

It has been suggested that unethical behavior by salespeople can result in dissatisfied customers, ultimately leading to decreased sales and lower profits for suppliers (Levy & Dubinsky, 1983). Similarly, a difference in the gap between buyers' and suppliers' perceptions of the degree of ethicality of the buyers' activities may result in actions on the suppliers' part that ultimately affect the satisfaction of buyers.

Research Question 7: How does the level of unethical activity affect the effectiveness of the global buyer-supplier relationship?

Along the same lines, significant gaps between the perceptions of buyers and their suppliers concerning the ethics of each's actions might result in decreased performance and effectiveness by the supplier. For example, buyers might experience reduced customer service and lower cost-effectiveness as a result of less ethical activity in the relationship, as both sides may be less inclined to commit to and take a long-term perspective of the buyer-supplier relationship (Chonko, Tanner, & Weeks, 1996). Both sides may begin to look out for their own firm, and put the goals of their individual firms ahead of the combined interests of the buyer-supplier dyad, at the expense of hurting the other party (Frazier, Spekman, & O'Neal, 1988) and ultimately the supply chain as a whole (Houlihan, 1985; Ellram & Cooper, 1990; Ellram, 1991).

The study's seven research questions are presented graphically in Figure 1. Next, the two dominant philosophies of modern ethics are briefly introduced, and a definition of unethical activities in buyer-supplier relationships is presented. Finally, the results from the focus group interviews and a set of survey questionnaires are used to answer the above research questions.

DEFINING ETHICS

There are two major current philosophical traditions in business ethics. Under the viewpoint of *deontology*, an activity could be defined as ethical if it is freely under-

FIGURE 1
FACTORS AFFECTING AND AFFECTED BY UNETHICAL PRACTICES

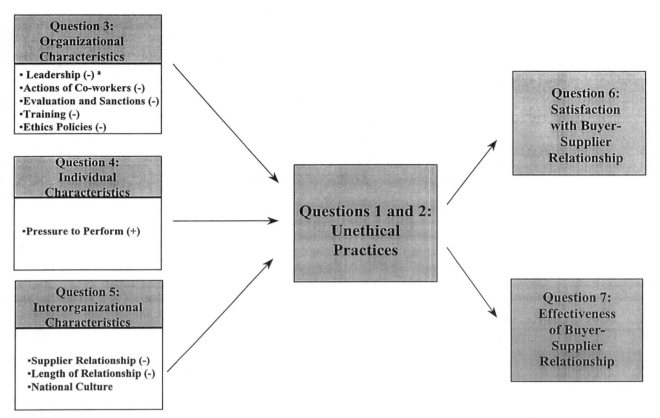

[a] A minus (plus) sign hypothesizes a negative (positive) relationship between a bulleted characteristic and unethical practices.

taken, available to all, injures no one, and benefits some. Based on this definition, activities such as writing specifications that favor a particular supplier, overestimating demand to gain volume concessions, and purposefully misleading a salesperson in a negotiation are practices that would be considered unethical by deontologists.

Under *utilitarianism* an activity is considered ethical and morally acceptable if a social cost/benefit analysis (the net of all benefits minus the net of all costs) yields a positive net result. Thus, activities that may hurt some parties are still considered ethical under this approach, because society as a whole benefits. Perhaps because of its grounding in economics, the utilitarian philosophy is the dominant philosophy among business managers (Fritzsche & Becker, 1983; Robin & Reidenbach, 1987).

The purpose of introducing these two philosophical frameworks is not to advocate one over the other, but rather to show that the list of possible ethical actions is significantly larger than the list of unethical ones. For this reason, the author concentrates on unethical activi-

ties in buyer-supplier relationships. For the purpose of this study, unethical activities are defined as **the specific set of actions taken within the buyer-supplier relationship that are considered unacceptable, inappropriate, or irresponsible by purchasing managers.**

By presenting this definition, the author admittedly takes an ethnocentric viewpoint by allowing American purchasing managers to define which activities are ethical and which are not. The survey findings will show, however, that the activities identified as unethical by American buyers were viewed in a similar fashion by their international suppliers.

Focus Group Interviews

The purpose of conducting focus group of interviews was to build upon the findings of the literature review and the preceding definition of unethical activities to further determine the range of possible activities that might comprise unethical behaviors in buyer-supplier relationships. Focus group interviews in particular were chosen so that attention could be shifted away from the interviewer toward the participants to encourage a brainstorming of ideas by participants (Calder, 1977). This is accomplished by establishing a permissive environment in which members generate ideas based in part on responding to the comments of other members in the group (Krueger, 1988). It is important to note, however, that the focus group interviews were also a carefully planned discussion that followed a structured questioning route (see Appendix A).

The focus group interviews were conducted with purchasing managers from companies that purchase from international suppliers. These firms represented a diverse group of industries, including consumer products, aerospace, pharmaceuticals, construction equipment, and foodstuffs. The literature review identified a wide range of activities that have been included under the general rubric of unethical behavior in buyer-supplier relationships. The interviews with purchasing managers identified many of the same activities, which are listed in Table 1.

Unethical Practices Identified through the Focus Group Interviews — The focus group participants unanimously agreed that lying to a supplier was explicitly unethical. The focus group discussions also complimented the findings from the literature review, which suggested there are a number of less tangible ways in which deception can occur. These activities include using ambiguous contract terms or other forms of communication to gain an advantage over the other party, exaggerating the seriousness of a problem to gain concessions, overestimating demand to gain volume discounts, over-

TABLE 1
UNETHICAL ACTIVITIES IDENTIFIED THROUGH THE LITERATURE REVIEW AND GROUP INTERVIEWS

- Using obscure contract terms to gain advantage over other the party (Felch, 1985)
- Writing specifications that favor a particular supplier (Felch, 1985)
- Exaggerating the seriousness of a problem to gain concessions (Rudelius & Buchholz, 1979; Dubinsky & Gwin, 1981; Trevisan, 1986; Janson, 1988)
- Allowing a supplier to rebid after the closing date (Rudelius & Buchholz, 1979; Dubinsky & Gwin, 1981; Trevisan, 1986; Janson, 1988)
- Allowing only certain suppliers to bid (Trevisan, 1986)
- Giving preference to suppliers preferred by top management (Trevisan, 1986; Puffer & McCarthy, 1995; Husted et al., 1996)
- Allowing the personalities of the supplier to affect decisions (Rudelius & Buchholz, 1979; Dubinsky & Gwin, 1981; Trevisan, 1986; Janson, 1988)
- Concocting/making up a second source of supply to gain an advantage over suppliers (Felch, 1985)
- Asking the other party for information about your competitors (Rudelius & Buchholz, 1979; Schlegelmilch & Robertson, 1995)
- Purposefully misleading the other party (Trevisan, 1986; van den Hengel, 1995)
- Using bribery (Donaldson, 1996; Puffer & McCarthy, 1995; Husted et al., 1996; Schlegelmilch & Robertson, 1995)
- Overestimating demand to gain volume discounts (van den Hengel, 1995)
- Soliciting quotations from suppliers who have little chance of success (Rudelius & Buchholz, 1979; Trevisan, 1986; Janson, 1988)
- Using "backdoor" selling techniques such as approaching personnel in engineering, manufacturing, or other departments outside of purchasing (Rudelius & Buchholz, 1979; Trevisan, 1986; Forker & Janson, 1990; Dubinsky & Gwin, 1981)
- Canceling purchase orders in progress and trying to avoid cancellation charges (Rudelius & Buchholz, 1979; Trevisan, 1986)
- Allowing a supplier to become dependent on the purchasing organization for most of its business (Trevisan, 1986; van den Hengel, 1995)
- Using small payments to facilitate international transactions (Donaldson, 1996; Puffer & McCarthy, 1995; Husted et al., 1996; Schlegelmilch & Robertson, 1995)
- Using less competitive prices or terms for buyers who purchase exclusively from the supplier (Dubinsky & Gwin, 1981)
- Increasing prices when there is a shortage of supply of the purchased material or product (Janson, 1988)
- Offering gifts in excess of nominal value (Schlegelmilch & Robertson, 1995; Felch, 1985)
- Overcommiting resources or production schedules (van den Hengel, 1995)

commiting resources or production schedules, or in any similar way misleading the other party.

Interviewees also unanimously agreed that breaking the law was unethical. From an international standpoint, the Foreign Corrupt Practices Act and the Omnibus Trade Act of 1988 regulate conditions under which payment may be made to foreign officials (Pitman & Sanford, 1994). The Acts make it illegal for American companies and their employees to make payments or give gifts of significant value to foreign officials. Bribery of a foreign official regarding a critical decision, such as allowing a firm to obtain or retain business, is illegal. However, other types of bribery, such as facilitating payments, *are legal.* Facilitating payments are bribes to lower-level officials that create an incentive to more promptly perform routine activities that would have been performed as part of their duties regardless of whether the payment was made. Examples of these routine activities include loading or unloading cargo, processing goods through customs, and processing other paperwork related to international trade.

Ethical actions mean more than just obeying the law or avoiding deceit. There are many other activities that, while not involving outright deception, were also considered by focus group participants to be potentially unethical. These activities include allowing personalities and friendships to influence decisions, accepting a bid or allowing a favored supplier to rebid after the closing date, canceling purchase orders in progress and trying to avoid cancellation charges, and asking the other party for proprietary information about competitors. Examples of proprietary information include price and cost data, proprietary knowledge concerning software and production processes, and suppliers' bids. Other unethical activities related to the competitive bidding process include writing specifications that favor a particular supplier, and soliciting quotations from suppliers who have little or no chance of success.

Interestingly, environmental or "green" purchasing, and activities dealing with human rights such as purchasing from suppliers that use child labor, were not brought out through the focus group interviews, and were rarely mentioned in the ethics literature. These activities are generally not thought of as ethical issues in particular, but rather considered within the broader context of corporate social responsibility. Finally, the majority of unethical buyer activities identified through the literature review and the focus group interviews were activities that could viably take place in both a domestic or international context, although the literature indicated that some of these activities might be more prevalent in international buyer-supplier relationships, such as bribery and facilitating payments.

Specific supplier activities identified as being unethical included increasing prices when there is a shortage of supply and knowingly overcommiting resources or production schedules. For example, Inland

Steel Chairman Rob Darnall notes that, "Time after time, we've had to say to our customers, 'No, we can't do that, we can't do everything that you want'"(Berry, 1995, pp. 2). Similarly, Inland has resisted the temptation to discontinue shipping steel to contract customers at lower prices when spot market prices have risen.

Other supplier activities that the focus group participants suggested may be unethical include using less competitive prices or terms for buyers who purchase exclusively from the supplier, and avoiding personnel in purchasing by approaching personnel in such departments as engineering or manufacturing. Bribery and the offering of gifts in excess of nominal value were identified as unethical activities that were perhaps more prevalent on an international scale.

While the focus group interviews helped to identify the range of possible activities that might comprise ethical issues in global buyer-supplier relationships, they do not allow researchers to generalize to the overall population of buyer-supplier relationships (McQuarrie & McIntyre, 1988). Another limitation of focus group interviews is that it is not possible to measure the influence of potential precursors of unethical activity such as a code of ethics or ethics training, nor the possible outcomes such as decreased effectiveness of and satisfaction with the buyer-supplier relationship. For these reasons, a set of survey questionnaires were sent to U.S. purchasing managers and their foreign suppliers.

Survey Response: Buyers

Buyer-respondents represented such wide-ranging industries as petroleum, aerospace, consumer products, pharmaceuticals, electronics, chemicals, foodstuffs, telecommunications, transportation, and metals. Other diverse industries included apparel, biotechnology, construction, financial services, and pulp and paper.

Respondents came from firms in manufacturing (80.0%), distribution and retail (5.4%) and other services (14.6%). Figure 2 shows that the respondents, individuals who had "close and frequent contact" with an international supplier, included personnel in a broad range of managerial levels ranging from buyers and materials specialists through directors and vice presidents.

The company sales figures and purchase volumes from the individual international suppliers suggest that the buyer respondents represent medium to large-size firms:

- Median Annual Sales: $1.8 billion
- Range of Annual Sales: $12 million to $30 billion
- Median Purchases from the International Supplier: $3 million
- Range of Purchases: $10,000 to $200 million

FIGURE 2
RESPONDENTS' POSITIONS IN THE BUYING FIRM

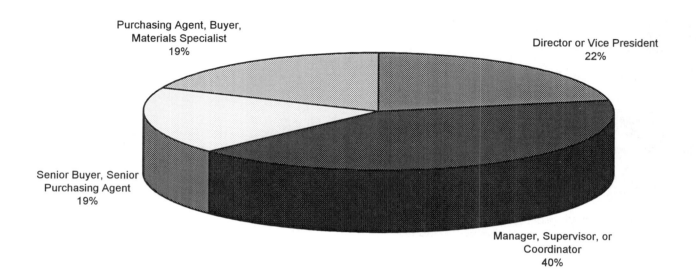

Purchasing Agent, Buyer,
Materials Specialist
19%

Director or Vice President
22%

Senior Buyer, Senior
Purchasing Agent
19%

Manager, Supervisor, or
Coordinator
40%

Survey Response: Suppliers

Respondents to the supplier questionnaire came from such diverse industries as aerospace (aircraft components and subassemblies), forgings and castings, chemicals, and electronics. Other products and services provided to buyers ranged from dehydrated vegetables to fiber optic cable to testing results. Most suppliers were in manufacturing industries (84.3%) with the remainder in distribution (9.7%) and other services (6.0%).

The overall supplier sales figures suggest that the supplier respondents represent a range of small to large-size firms:

- Median Annual Sales: $ 65 million
- Range of Annual Sales: $ 2 million to $125 billion

Next, the results from the analysis of the survey responses are introduced and used to answer the study's research questions.

Research Question 1: What are the specific activities that encompass ethical issues in global buyer-supplier relationships?

Unethical Activities: Buyers — Exploratory factor analysis (EFA) was used to determine whether the survey questions in Table 1 relating to buyer activities were actually measuring a single-dimension construct. If not, the EFA would then aid in identifying the number and nature of the underlying dimensions making up the ethics construct. A more detailed explanation of the EFA used for this study is presented in Appendix D.

The EFA suggests that the unethical activity of buyers actually consists of two distinct dimensions. The first dimension includes survey questions addressing activities such as using obscure contract terms to gain advantage over the supplier and purposefully misleading the supplier. The first dimension seems to consist of activities involving deception, and was subsequently termed *deceitful practices.*

Five survey questions were related to the second dimension. Here, the items included somewhat more subtle activities such as allowing suppliers to rebid after the closing date and giving preference to suppliers preferred by top management. The second factor was consequently termed *subtle practices.*

TABLE 2
BUYER ACTIVITIES

Deceitful Practices

(Currently, our purchasing function) [a]
- Invents (makes up) a second source of supply to gain competitive advantage
- Uses obscure contract terms to gain an advantage over suppliers
- Exaggerates the seriousness of a problem to gain concessions
- Purposefully misleads a salesperson in a negotiation

Subtle Practices

(Currently, our purchasing function) [a]
- Gives preference to suppliers preferred by top management
- Allows personalities of the supplier to impact decisions
- Writes specifications that favor a particular supplier

[a] These items were measured on a 5-point Likert scale where 1 = Never and 5 = Always.

The two dimensions of unethical buyer activities were next subjected to a confirmatory factor analysis (CFA). The survey questions in Table 2 (Deceitful Practices and Subtle Practices) resulted in a statistically meaningful two-factor model. Due to the small sample size, the confirmatory factor analysis was conducted on the same sample of buyers as was the exploratory factor analysis. The use of the same sample for both analyses can result in the capitalization of chance since the data sets were identical. As a result, a second confirmatory factor analysis was conducted using the suppliers' answers to the same survey questions shown in Table 2. A statistically similar pattern of results was found regarding the suppliers' perceptions of the buyers activities.

Unethical Activities: Suppliers — An EFA of the survey questions relating to supplier activities indicated that these questions represented a single-dimension construct, and this was corroborated by a CFA of the responses from purchasing managers. A second CFA, using the suppliers' answers to the same survey questions presented in Table 3, resulted in a statistically similar pattern of results.

It is important to note that questionnaire items not included in the final scales in Tables 2 and 3 might very well be relevant in some firms, including bribery and the use of facilitating payments. In other firms, buyers may not have the opportunity to be involved in these activities to a great extent. For example, buyers may arrange transportation services through an importer-exporter, composite office, or other third-party, that in turn deals directly with government officials, customs, and regulations. Finally, managers must continually monitor and assess the ethicality of actions of purchasing personnel, as the perceptions of what is considered to be ethical and acceptable behavior might change over time (Trevisan, 1986; Wood, 1991).

One possibility is that buyers and suppliers view the ethicality of the identified activities similarly because there are fundamental, core values that cross cultures. For example, Husted et al. (1996) compare both the atti-

TABLE 3
SUPPLIER ACTIVITIES

Currently, the supplier: [a]
- Uses less competitive prices or terms for buyers who purchase exclusively from the supplier
- Uses backdoor selling techniques (such as approaching personnel in engineering, manufacturing, or other departments outside of purchasing)
- Increases prices when there is a shortage of supply of the purchased material or product
- Offers gifts in excess of nominal value
- Asks us for information about their competitors
- Uses obscure contract terms to gain an advantage over us
- Lies to or grossly misleads us in a negotiation
- Knowingly over-commits resources or production schedules

[a] These items were measured on a 5-point Likert scale where 1 = Never and 5 = Always.

21

tudes and moral reasoning of MBA students in Mexico, Spain, and the United States. The authors found that the attitudes of the students from all three countries are similar in terms of identifying the same issues as being unethical. Still, this is probably an overly simplistic and somewhat inadequate explanation that may be due to the preselection of that study's subjects into MBA programs.

It is also possible that there is congruence between buyers and suppliers, in terms of their identification of unethical activities, because norms and expectations of ethics have been established and communicated as part of their particular business relationship, as well as through international suppliers' prior relationships with other American customers. Some of the study's participants suggested that, in today's global economy, foreign suppliers generally understand the activities and behaviors that American buyers consider to be acceptable and unacceptable. It is important to note, however, that these findings are based only on the perceptions of American buyers and their foreign suppliers. Interviews with purchasing managers suggested that when purchasing occurs entirely offshore, such as purchasing in a foreign country for a plant or facility in that country, activities may occur that would not be acceptable in the United States. Further, the study's participants proposed that some of the activities deemed unethical were not necessarily unacceptable to them, if they occurred entirely within a foreign country or culture that considers the activities to be both legal and ethical.

These statistical findings also corroborate the assertions of Dobler and Burt (1996), who suggest that the differences between the ethical issues involved with international versus domestic purchasing are really more a matter of degree than absolute disparities. Activities such as bribery and the use of grease payments, which have typically been associated with international transactions, were not found to load on either of the two buyer factors or the supplier activities. This suggests that these activities are not nearly as prevalent on the part of buyers as might have been the case in the past. The factor analysis using the supplier data yielded similar results, suggesting that international suppliers realize these activities are unacceptable when dealing with American buyers.

The CFAs showed there was agreement between buyers and their suppliers concerning whether and how they viewed the ethicality of certain activities. The second research question asks whether there are in turn differences in the perceived levels of these activities between the buyer and supplier groups. For example, while buyers and suppliers may agree on whether certain activities are unethical, there could still be differences between how the buyer views his/her level of involvement in these activities and how the supplier views the buyer's involvement in those same acts. At the same time, differences may exist in how a buyer and supplier

view the supplier's level of involvement in unethical activities.

Research Question 2: Are there differences between the perceptions of buyers and suppliers regarding the level of unethical behavior in the relationships?

A two-group discriminant analysis was used to answer this question, using the survey questions in Tables 2 and 3. A discriminant analysis was employed so that the researcher could determine whether a significant *overall* difference existed for each of the two dimensions of buyer activities and for the supplier activities. Table 4 displays the unweighted group means for each of the survey questions representing the various buyer and supplier activities. The tables show that the Wilks' Lambda values ranged from 0.7112 to 0.9093, and were all significant ($p < 0.0001$). This means that there are significant overall differences between the perceptions of buyers and their suppliers for the deceitful and subtle practices of the buyers and for the supplier activities as well.

The univariate F ratios for each set of the survey questions are also shown in Table 4. These F-values indicate that significant differences exist for many of the *individual* survey items as well. The gaps between buyers' and suppliers' perceptions on the individual survey questions are displayed visually in Figures 3-5. There are a number of potential reasons to explain why these large gaps exist. Some examples are given below.

Why Do These Gaps Occur? — Significant gaps existed between buyers' and suppliers' perceptions concerning most of the activities comprising deceitful practices. It is possible that buyers are not accurately communicating their intentions to their suppliers. For example, suppliers may believe that a buyer is exaggerating the seriousness of a problem to gain price concessions or improve service levels, while the buyer may believe that the problem legitimately exists. Similarly, the buyer may in fact be considering a second source of supply unbeknownst to the supplier.

The degree to which an organization is open and allows purchasing managers to function in a professional manner might also affect the gaps between buyers' and suppliers' perceptions. One interviewee related a story of working in the past for another company in which the buying firm's CEO was golfing with the president of a supplier company, who said, "My one division down here has tried to get in to do business with your company for the last six years and we just can't get in. What's the problem?" The next day, a phone call was made from the buying firm's CEO to the vice president of purchasing, asking about the supplier. This was in turn filtered down to the next level. A very specific and concise answer was returned to the CEO, stating that "we don't do business with the supplier for the following reasons..." This

TABLE 4
DISCRIMINANT ANALYSIS OF ETHICAL PRACTICES

Deceitful Practices

Questionnaire Item	Mean: Buyer Firms	Mean: Supplier Firms	Univariate F Ratio
Invents (makes up a second source) ...	1.33	1.98	27.70 ****
Uses obscure contract terms ...	1.22	1.33	1.94
Exaggerates the seriousness of a problem ...	1.52	1.80	8.22 **
Purposefully misleads a salesperson ...	1.17	1.36	8.05 **

Wilks' Lambda = .8715 (p<.0001)

Subtle Practices

Questionnaire Item	Mean: Buyer Firms	Mean: Supplier Firms	Univariate F Ratio
Gives preference to suppliers preferred by ...	2.27	2.81	12.74 ***
Allows personalities of supplies to impact ...	2.01	1.82	2.17
Writes specifications that favor a particular ...	1.69	1.71	0.02

Wilks' Lambda = .9093 (p<.0001)

Supplier Activities

Questionnaire Item	Mean: Buyer Firms	Mean: Supplier Firms	Univariate F Ratio
Uses less competitive terms or prices ...	1.81	1.63	2.48
Uses backdoor selling techniques ...	1.70	2.00	4.98 *
Increases prices when there is a shortage ...	2.16	1.98	1.40
Offers gifts in excess of nominal ...	1.22	1.77	27.54 ****
Asks us for information about competitors ...	1.98	2.38	8.81 **
Uses obscure contract terms ...	1.34	1.13	8.69 **
Lies or grossly misleads ...	1.21	1.05	8.40 **
Knowingly over-commits resources	1.60	1.44	2.68

Wilks' Lambda = .7112 (p<.0001)

* p<.05
** p<.005
*** p<.001
**** p<.0001
NOTE: Complete scale items are displayed in Appendix D, Table 12.

example illustrates a significant difference in company philosophies. In some companies, the CEO's inquiry might have been perceived as a request, and the supplier given at least some business as a result of that inquiry.

As a final example, some suppliers might offer gifts in excess of nominal value because this is part of their culture and customs. Buyers in some American companies accept these gifts because they realize that the suppliers are giving these gifts as a sign of respect, rather than seeking to gain influence. Comments by purchasing managers suggested, however, that these gifts were almost always donated or in some other fashion given to the purchasing firm, rather than to the individual buyer.

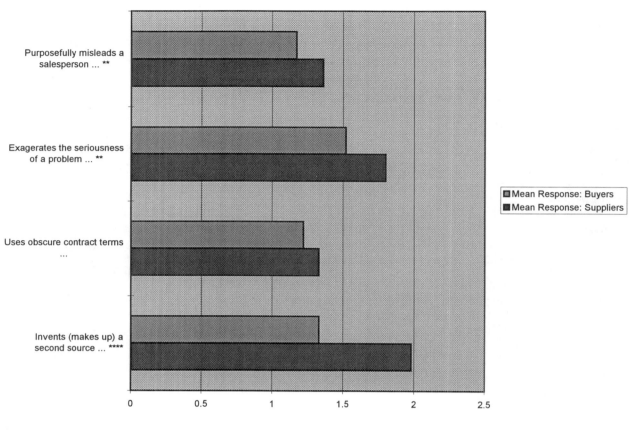

FIGURE 3
DECEITFUL PRACTICES: BUYERS' VERSUS SUPPLIERS' PERCEPTIONS

1 = Never; 5 = Always
*p<0.05; **p<0.005; ***p<0.001; ****p<0.0001

As a result, buyers may not consider this to be a gift in excess of nominal value because they do not personally receive the gift.

Perhaps just as important as discerning how these gaps occur is understanding how significant gaps between buyers' and supplier's perceptions of each other's ethical activities can in turn impact the effectiveness of and satisfaction with the buyer-supplier relationship. These issues are explored in research questions 6 and 7.

Research Question 3: What are the organizational factors that affect the ethicality of global buyer-supplier relationships?

The survey questions used to measure Leadership, Actions of Co-workers, Evaluation, and Ethics Training were measured on five-point Likert scales (see Appendix B). Multiple regression analysis was used to examine the relationship between these variables and the two dimensions of unethical purchasing behavior (deceitful prac-

tices and subtle practices). Analysis of variance was used to examine the seven yes/no survey questions that asked purchasing managers about ethics policies in their firms.

Because there were no *a priori* hypotheses as to which of these four independent variables should be most strongly related to each of the dimensions of unethical purchasing practices, a forward stepwise regression procedure was run. Forward stepwise regression enters the independent variable which explains the largest amount of variance in the dependent variable. Additional independent variables are then entered one at a time into the model if they can explain significant variance in the dependent variable, above and beyond what was explained by the variable(s) already in the model. At each stage the stepwise procedure also examines whether the variables already in the model remain significant; if not, they are dropped. Forward selection and backward selection procedures were also run in order to assess model fit (readers unfamiliar with these procedures are referred to Neter, Wasserman, & Kutner, 1990).

FIGURE 4
SUBTLE PRACTICES: BUYERS' VERSUS SUPPLIERS' PERCEPTIONS

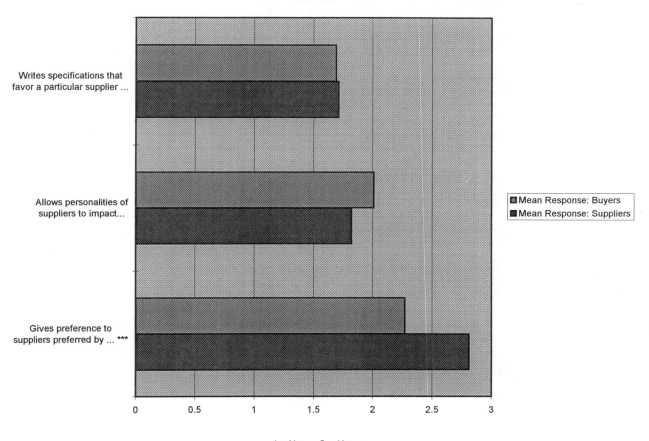

1 = Never; 5 = Always
*p<0.05; **p<0.005; ***p<0.001; ****p<0.0001

Deceitful Practices — A regression of leadership, actions of co-workers, evaluation, and training on the deceitful practices dimension of potential buyer activities indicated that none of these four variables were significantly related to the deceitful practices dimension. However, an analysis of variance, using the seven survey questions representing ethics policies found that communicating ethics standards to suppliers and having an ethics hotline in place were significantly related to the deceitful practices dimension ($p<0.01$, adjusted $R^2=0.10$). The results from this analysis of variance are shown in Table 5.

The results suggest that the activities comprising deceitful practices are not affected by the actions and examples of either leadership or co-workers, nor are they influenced by formal evaluation or training in ethical matters. One purchasing manager suggested that the type of purchasing manager who will tend to rely heavily on deceitful practices will use these regardless of the amount of training he receives: "It's a personal inade-quacy that's rewarded by short-term recognition but long-term failure." However, buyers appear to be dissuaded from undertaking these activities when firms formally communicate their ethical standards to suppliers and have a hotline in place through which these unethical activities can be reported. These findings corroborate the assertions of other researchers (Rudelius & Buchholz, 1979; van den Hengel, 1995).

In addition, the presence of a code of ethics was not significantly related to the deceitful practices activities. However, the influence of a code of ethics is probably at least somewhat dependent on the firm's commitment to the code. This commitment can be demonstrated in a number of ways, including communicating the code to suppliers and having an ethics hotline to report violations of the code. It appears that buyers who might be tempted to engage in deceitful practices will do so regardless of the amount of training they have received, or how ethically their managers act. Instead, a fear of being reported by either an informed supplier or personnel in the buying

FIGURE 5
SUPPLIER ACTIVITIES: BUYERS' VERSUS SUPPLIERS' PERCEPTIONS

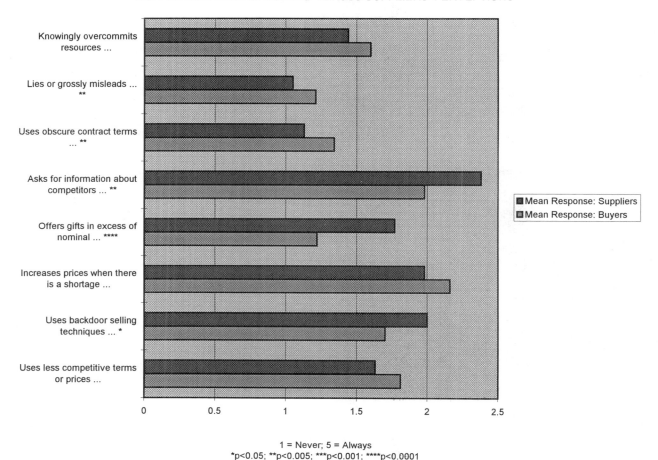

1 = Never; 5 = Always
*p<0.05; **p<0.005; ***p<0.001; ****p<0.0001

TABLE 5
KEY ORGANIZATIONAL CHARACTERISTICS AFFECTING DECEITFUL PRACTICES

SIGNIFICANT NEGATIVELY CORRELATED ETHICS POLICIES DETERMINED THROUGH ANALYSIS OF VARIANCE

FACTOR	p-VALUE
We periodically communicate our ethical standards to suppliers	0.0249
My firm has an ethics hotline	0.0049

F-VALUE: 4.46, p<.01
R-Square: .096

organization may dissuade buyers from engaging in these behaviors.

Finally, while not an issue assessed as part of this study, it would seem important that purchasing managers do not ethnocentrically and insensitively communicate their ethics codes to suppliers, but rather carefully explain any potential discrepancies within the context of the relevance and importance of these issues to other cultures (Frederick, 1991; Rowan & Campbell, 1983).

Subtle Practices — A second regression of leadership, actions of co-workers, evaluation, and training on the subtle practices dimension of potential buyer activities was made. Forward selection, backward elimination, and forward stepwise regression procedures, using toler-

TABLE 6
KEY ORGANIZATIONAL CHARACTERISTICS AFFECTING SUBTLE PRACTICES

SIGNIFICANT NEGATIVELY CORRELATED ETHICS POLICIES DETERMINED THROUGH MULTIPLE REGRESSION ANALYSIS

FACTOR	p-VALUE
Evaluation	0.0002
Training	0.0063

F-VALUE: 8.98, p<.001
Adjusted R-Square: .109

Note: The survey questions used to measure Evaluation and Training are displayed in Appendix D, Table 12.

ance levels of 0.05, all resulted in the retention of the same two independent variables. The results, shown in Table 6, suggest that evaluation and training significantly reduced the level of unethical activities comprising the subtle practices dimension. The analysis of variance using the seven ethics policies variables found that none of the seven variables were significantly related to subtle practices.

Whereas engaging in deceitful practices is often more clearly unethical, the activities that encompass subtle practices tend to fall into a gray area. Training appears to help educate buyers and make them aware of these more subtle ethical issues. This may not only be useful for new and inexperienced purchasing managers, but also for more experienced personnel who find themselves in unfamiliar situations. Similarly, including ethical issues in a buyer's formal evaluations can help to reinforce material and policies covered during training.

Research Question 4: How do a buyer's and supplier's pressure to perform affect the ethicality of global buyer-supplier relationships?

The pressures experienced by buyers were not significantly related to either the deceitful practices (p=0.83) or subtle practices (p=0.79) dimensions of unethical activities. Pressures felt by the supplier respondents were also not significantly related to unethical activities on the supplier's part (p=0.25).

One possible explanation for these findings is that savvy buyers realize that engaging in unethical practices will hurt them professionally in the long run. First, their company's reputation will be damaged. If an agreement is entered into unethically, or if unethical actions occur during the course of a contract, this is not a win-win transaction or even a win-lose deal, but rather a lose-lose situation. When the contract opens up again, the supplier may choose not to do business with the buying firm. Further, as suggested by one of the study's participants, "pretty soon word gets out and everyone is adding 10 percent into their pricing because of the buying company's unethical reputation. It's the cost of doing business, and suppliers figure that out."

Many buyers probably also realize that unethical behaviors will hurt them personally. It's likely that buyers who act unethically towards suppliers will not only lose the trust of those suppliers, but also of employees inside of the buying firm with whom they interact. Similarly, if a salesperson acts unethically, he will probably lose the trust of, and consequently the business from, the buyer. Respondents indicated that it's a "small world" and that an unethical reputation can spread quickly, not only within a company but throughout companies in an industry.

Research Question 5: What external factors affect the ethicality of global buyer-supplier relationships?

Regression analysis found no relationship between unethical practices and either the nature of the buyer-supplier relationship or the length of time the relationship had existed. In addition, an analysis of variance did not indicate a significant relationship between the supplier's nationality and unethical practices of either the buyer or supplier.

These results suggest that the type of relationship a buyer has with a supplier does not affect the degree of unethical behavior in the relationship. Similarly, the length of time that the relationship has been in existence does not appear to affect the level of unethical activities. It appears that buyers and suppliers will engage in unethical practices (whether to a great extent, not at all, or somewhere in between) regardless of these factors.

A supplier's nationality was also unrelated to the level of unethical activities found in the buyer-supplier relationship. Again, the range of behaviors and activities that are considered to be unethical by American purchasing managers appear to be well communicated to and understood by their international suppliers. As was noted earlier, the surveyed suppliers have probably gained this understanding not only through their current relationships with the surveyed buyers, but also through their prior relationships with other U.S. buying firms. While differences in ethical values almost certainly do still exist *within* countries, this too may change as even local business continues to become increasingly international in character.

The results from examining the last two research questions are presented next. These research questions investigate the potential influence of unethical activities (and the differences between how buyers and suppliers view these activities) on how satisfied buyers are with their supplier relationships and how effectively buyers believe suppliers are performing.

Research Questions 6 and 7: How does the level of unethical activity affect satisfaction with the global buyer-supplier relationship? How does the level of unethical activity affect the effectiveness of the global buyer-supplier relationship?

A regression analysis was run to determine the impact of deceitful practices, subtle practices, and sup-

plier activities (all from the buyer's perspective) on the buyer's satisfaction with the supplier relationship. The results shown in Table 7 indicate that a significant, negative relationship exists between the supplier's level of unethical activities and the buyer's satisfaction with the supplier relationship. This means that as the unethical activities of a supplier increase, the buyer's satisfaction decreases.

A similar regression analysis was run to determine how deceitful practices, subtle practices, and supplier activities affect the effectiveness of the buyer-supplier relationship. The results from this second regression analysis are presented in Table 8. Again, the level of unethical activities of the supplier is significantly related to how effectively the buyer believes the supplier is performing.

Thus, buyers who perceived higher levels of unethical activities on the part of suppliers were less satisfied with their relationship with the suppliers. Buyers also believed that suppliers who were more involved in unethical activities were less effective. As one participant suggested, "You kind of wonder what they are hiding now that they have to resort to this type of activity in

TABLE 7
BUYER'S VIEWPOINT: KEY ETHICS DIMENSIONS AFFECTING BUYERS' SATISFACTION WITH THE SUPPLIER

SIGNIFICANT NEGATIVELY CORRELATED ETHICS DIMENIONS DETERMINED THROUGH MULTIPLE REGRESSION ANALYSIS

DIMENSION	p-VALUE
DECEITFUL PRACTICES	0.3185
SUBTLE PRACTICES	0.7985
SUPPLIER ACTIVITIES	0.0010

F-VALUE: 5.060, p<.005
Adjusted R-Square: .09

TABLE 8
BUYER'S VIEWPOINT: KEY ETHICS DIMENSIONS AFFECTING EFFECTIVENESS OF THE BUYER-SUPPLIER RELATIONSHIP

SIGNIFICANT NEGATIVELY CORRELATED ETHICS DIMENIONS DETERMINED THROUGH MULTIPLE REGRESSION ANALYSIS

DIMENSION	p-VALUE
DECEITFUL PRACTICES	0.1731
SUBTLE PRACTICES	0.5653
SUPPLIER ACTIVITIES	0.0431

F-VALUE: 2.846, p<.05
Adjusted R-Square: .04

order to stay on as a supplier or become a supplier." Similarly, a participant related an account of a salesperson who lied to a buyer's manager to hide production problems at the supplier's plant. This not only resulted in lower satisfaction experienced by the buying firm, but also reduced the buyer's perception of the supplier's performance in terms of service, quality, and price.

Finally, difference or "gap" scores were calculated between buyers' perceptions and their suppliers' perceptions of deceitful practices, subtle practices, and supplier actions. A second set of regression analyses were run between these independent variables and both the buyers' satisfaction with (Research Question 6) and their perception of the effectiveness of (Research Question 7) the buyer-supplier relationship. The regression analyses resulted in a significant relationship between the gaps in perceptions regarding deceitful practices and the buyer's satisfaction with the relationship, as shown in Table 9. No significant relationship was found between any of the "gap" scores of ethics dimensions and how effectively the supplier was performing.

These findings suggest that when gaps exist between a buyer's and supplier's perceptions concerning unethical activities that involve outright deceit, this affects the buyer's satisfaction with the relationship. This corresponds to earlier input from study participants, who indicated that although those engaged in deceitful practices may achieve short-term gains, they will be less satisfied with the relationship in the long run, as suppliers refuse to renew contracts and continue with the relationship.

CONCLUSIONS

The findings of this research point to a number of factors that can affect the level of purchasing's involvement in unethical activities. Unethical behaviors in the buyer-supplier relationship can affect satisfaction and even a buyer's perception of a supplier's effectiveness, but this is not true of all types of unethical activities. Finally, the activities that are viewed as being unethical are consistent across national cultures, at least when foreign suppliers are dealing with American buyers. These findings are summarized below:

1. Foreign suppliers identified the same activities as being unethical that U.S. buyers did. One explanation for these buyers and suppliers judging the ethicality of the identified activities in the same manner is because there are fundamental, core values that cross cultures. Perhaps a more realistic explanation is that similarities between buyers and suppliers in terms of identifying unethical activities are likely due to the norms and expectations of ethics that have been established and communicated as part of the buyer-supplier relationship, as well as through an international supplier's prior affiliations with other American companies.

2. The ethical issues involved in the relationships between American buyers and their foreign suppliers appear to be the same as those found in domestic sourcing. For example, analysis of the survey data found that activities such as bribery and the use of "grease" (facilitating) payments, which have typically been associated with international transactions, were not included in either of the two buyer categories of unethical practices or unethical supplier activities. This suggests that U.S. buyers are not engaging in these activities as prevalently as they might have in the past. Further, international suppliers appear to realize that these activities are unacceptable when dealing with American buyers.

3. While the surveyed buyers and suppliers identified the same dimensions of unethical actions, significant differences did exist between buyers' and suppliers' perceptions regarding how involved each believed the other to be in these activities. It is important to realize that even the appearance of an unethical action can affect a party's perception of how ethical the other party's behavior really is. For example, a supplier may believe that it can meet a promised production

TABLE 9
GAPS BETWEEN BUYERS' AND SUPPLIERS' VIEWPOINTS: KEY ETHICS DIMENSIONS AFFECTING BUYER SATISFACTION WITH THE SUPPLIER

SIGNIFICANT NEGATIVELY CORRELATED ETHICS DIMENIONS DETERMINED THROUGH MULTIPLE REGRESSION ANALYSIS

DIMENSION	p-VALUE
DECEITFUL PRACTICES	0.0148
SUBTLE PRACTICES	0.5402
SUPPLIER ACTIVITIES	0.2549

F-VALUE: 3.536, p<.01
Adjusted R-Square: .09

schedule, but then experience production delays and be unable to deliver as promised. While the supplier may not believe that it has acted in an unethical manner, the buyer may perceive that the supplier has knowingly, and thus unethically, over-committed resources or production schedules. It is thus important for both buyers and suppliers to openly communicate their intentions and all relevant transaction details, in order to minimize the "gaps" that can occur between how each party perceives the other.

4. The deceitful practices of buyers are minimized when companies communicate ethics policies to suppliers and have an ethics hotline in place. Other organizational factors, such as top management "walking the talk" or providing training appear to have no influence on the degree to which purchasing managers are involved in this dimension of buyer activities. The only practical deterrent appears to be the fear of getting caught or reported, which would be more likely to occur when policies are communicated to suppliers and when firms have an ethics hotline in place.

5. The deeper, less obvious activities comprising buyer's subtle practices were affected by both ethics training and the inclusion of ethical issues in an employee's formal evaluation. Ethics training can help make new, inexperienced, and even seasoned buyers more aware of these less obvious, unethical behaviors. In turn, including ethical issues as a part of a buyer's formal evaluations can help to reinforce material and policies covered during training.

6. One might assume that buyers who are under pressure to perform and who want to advance in their careers may choose to engage in unethical practices. This is not the case. Similarly, there is no relationship between pressures felt by foreign supplier representatives and their involvement in unethical activities. It appears that both buyers and suppliers realize that employing unethical practices will at best result in short-term success, but will inevitably culminate in damage to both their careers and the buyer-supplier relationship.

7. The researcher found no relationship between the supplier's nationality and the level of unethical activity in the buyer-supplier relationship. One explanation for this finding is that the behaviors and activities considered to be unethical by American purchasing managers have been well communicated to and are understood to be unethical by their foreign suppliers. Norms and expectations regarding ethics may have also been established through a foreign supplier's prior relationships with other U.S. buying firms. It is important to note that these findings apply only to U.S. buyers and their foreign suppliers. Interviews with purchasing managers suggest that different scenarios may exist when purchasing occurs outside of the United States, for a foreign-based plant or subsidiary.

8. The author also found no link between unethical practices and either the length or type of relationship that exists between the buyer and supplier. Once norms and behaviors are established in a relationship, it is unlikely that time alone will change those practices. Similarly, the type of relationships that buyers have with their suppliers is not related to the level of unethical behavior found in those relationships. Apparently, if purchasing managers or suppliers decide to act unethically, they will do so regardless of the type of relationship they have established with the other firm. Conversely, firms that choose to conduct business in an ethical manner will do so regardless of whether the relationship consists of a one-time transaction, a long-term contract, or a strategic alliance.

9. Buyers who were least satisfied with the buyer-supplier relationship were those who perceived their suppliers to be the most involved in unethical practices. Buyers were also the least satisfied if their own organizations were involved in deceitful practices. While deception may allow buyers to achieve short-term gains, they will be less satisfied with the relationship in the long-run, as suppliers increase prices or refuse to renew contracts.

10. When buyers perceive suppliers are involved in unethical practices, they believe that suppliers are performing less effectively. Buyers begin to wonder whether suppliers are trying to mask problems with production or quality, and believe that performance is reduced in terms of service and price.

Limitations and Suggestions for Future Research

The literature review showed that there has been a lack of a consistent approach to measuring ethical performance in purchasing and sales situations, as well as among businesses in general (Gatewood & Carroll, 1991). The development of a set of reliable and valid scales to measure unethical activities in buyer-supplier relationships provides an initial contribution in this area. An attempt was made to broadly define the relevant ethical issues within the relationships of U.S. buyers and their foreign suppliers. This was accomplished by integrating the findings from an extensive literature review with those of focus group interviews of purchasing practitioners, combined with a survey of both purchasing managers and their suppliers.

Purchasing managers from multiple industries were sampled in order to arrive at a sufficiently large sample size. Past research has suggested that responses can vary across purchasing and sales settings (Churchill, et al., 1985; Weitz, 1981). Neither the buy type nor industry were controlled for in the present study, and it is possible that ethical activities, their antecedents, and their consequences may vary among industries and buy types. Future research should examine the potential differences that may exist among industries, as well as categories of buying such as commodities versus make-to-buy and strategic purchases versus MRO procurement.

This study examined the matched perspectives of purchasing managers and suppliers. This allowed the author to not only examine the perspectives of American purchasing firms, but to also compare these perspectives to those of their foreign suppliers. The author is unaware of any other study that has used such a 'dyadic' perspective to examine ethical issues in buyer-supplier relationships. However, like many other studies that have employed a dyadic methodology, the number of matched buyer-supplier responses was relatively small.

While the 88 matched buyer-supplier surveys may seem small, this number is actually higher than average for this type of research method, in which matched responses are solicited across organizations using a set of mail surveys. For example, over a five-year period in the *Journal of Marketing,* the average number of matched buyer-supplier surveys reported for this type of methodology was 51. Like Hendrick and Ellram (1993), the researcher decided to sacrifice a potentially larger response from purchasing firms for a smaller but richer and more insightful response that also included the perspectives of suppliers.

Finally, one conclusion from the research is that buyers and their suppliers identified the same sets of activities as being unethical. It is important to note that this research examined the interactions of American purchasing managers and their foreign suppliers. Additional research is needed to see whether these findings hold across other international purchasing situations, when both the buyer and supplier are located outside of the United States.

APPENDIX A: FOCUS GROUP QUESTIONING ROUTE •

INTRODUCTION

We're here today to discuss ethical issues in purchasing. I want to start by saying that there are no right or wrong answers, but rather differing points of view. Please share your point of view even if it differs from what others have to say. I am just as interested in negative comments as positive comments; both can be very helpful.

QUESTIONING ROUTE

Looking back on your experiences as a buyer (purchasing executive), how would you define unethical behavior in purchasing?

Based on your experiences, what are some specific activities that you consider to be unethical behavior in purchasing?

Next I want to focus on ethical issues in an international context. Again, based on your experiences, what are some issues/activities that you consider to be unethical behavior in purchasing?

Think back to the last time that you were faced with an ethical issue in an international context, where your values did not mesh with those of the supplier. How did you deal with this situation?

> Probe: If the respondent cannot think of an example of the values not meshing, ask for any other ethical situation with a foreign supplier.

What aspect of your company most influences the ethicality of your behavior?

> Probe: Ethics statement, culture, top management support (use just one or two to "get the ball rolling" *if* necessary. Rotate order among groups to avoid bias)

Think about your dealings with an international supplier. Do you think that the culture of the supplier's country affected the way that the supplier viewed ethics? If so, how?

How might unethical practices affect your relationship with a supplier?

I have a list of activities which were identified through a review of the literature as comprising ethical issues in purchasing or in terms of general management. I would like to give you a few minutes to review this list and give me your insights. In particular, are there any issues that you can think of which are not on the list but should be included, and just as important, are there any issues included on the list that should be omitted? Also, is there any wording which is unclear?

Note: The questioning route was developed through brainstorming sessions with other academics and the input of the study's industry advisory group, and was pretested with a separate group of academics.

APPENDIX B: A SURVEY OF PURCHASING'S INVOLVEMENT IN INTERNATIONAL SOURCING: BUYER SURVEY •

This survey is being conducted by a researcher for the Center for Advanced Purchasing Studies. Your responses will be used to assess ethical issues in international buyer-supplier relationships. It is extremely important that you answer all questions regarding your firm's activities as *accurately* as possible. Your responses will remain *strictly confidential.*

Please answer *all* questions. If you are not sure of an answer to a question, please provide your *best* estimate.

Thank you for your help.

INSTRUCTIONS

1. Please select a single supplier outside of the U.S. and Canada with whom you have the closest and most frequent contact.

2. Please write *your company's name* at the **top of page 2 of the supplier questionnaire,** and promptly forward the supplier questionnaire to the supplier you have chosen.

3. Please fill-out the attached, self-addressed, stamped **postcard** with the chosen *supplier's* name and address and with *your firm's* name and address, and return the postcard to us.

4. Please complete and return this questionnaire in the self-addressed envelope. We will be happy to send you a summary of the results; simply include a business card with the completed survey. Thank you for your participation.

If you have any questions, please don't hesitate to call:

Craig R. Carter
Assistant Professor of International Purchasing
Center For Advanced Purchasing Studies
2055 East Centennial Circle
P.O. Box 22160
Tempe, AZ 85285-2160
(602) 752-2277

The second survey has been sent to (*name of supplier*): _____

This first set of questions explores the activities of *your firm's purchasing function* (not necessarily yourself) in dealing with the international supplier. Please circle your answers.

Currently, our *purchasing function:*	Never	Seldom	Occasionally	Often	Always
Allows a supplier to rebid after the closing date	1	2	3	4	5
Allows only certain suppliers to bid	1	2	3	4	5
Gives preference to suppliers preferred by top management	1	2	3	4	5
Allows personalities of the supplier to impact decisions	1	2	3	4	5
Writes specifications that favor a particular supplier	1	2	3	4	5
Invents (makes up) a second source of supply to gain competitive advantage	1	2	3	4	5
Asks suppliers for information about our competitors	1	2	3	4	5
Uses obscure contract terms to gain an advantage over suppliers	1	2	3	4	5
Exaggerates the seriousness of a problem to gain concessions	1	2	3	4	5
Purposefully misleads a salesperson in a negotiation	1	2	3	4	5
Uses bribery when dealing in foreign markets	1	2	3	4	5
Overestimates demand to gain volume discounts	1	2	3	4	5
Solicits quotations from suppliers who have little chance of success	1	2	3	4	5
Shows bias against suppliers who use "backdoor" selling techniques such as approaching personnel in engineering, manufacturing, or other departments outside of purchasing	1	2	3	4	5
Cancels purchase orders in progress and tries to avoid cancellation charges	1	2	3	4	5
Allows a supplier to become dependent on the purchasing organization for most of its business	1	2	3	4	5
Uses small payments to facilitate international transactions	1	2	3	4	5

This next set of questions asks about various activities of the international supplier. Please circle your answer.

Currently, the *supplier:*	Never	Seldom	Occasionally	Often	Always
Uses less competitive prices or terms for buyers who purchase exclusively from the supplier	1	2	3	4	5
Uses backdoor selling techniques	1	2	3	4	5
Increases prices when there is a shortage of supply of the purchased material or product	1	2	3	4	5
Offers gifts in excess of nominal value	1	2	3	4	5
Asks us for information about their competitors	1	2	3	4	5
Uses obscure contract terms to gain an advantage over us	1	2	3	4	5
Uses bribery when dealing with us	1	2	3	4	5
Exaggerates the seriousness of a problem to gain concessions	1	2	3	4	5
Lies to or grossly misleads us in a negotiation	1	2	3	4	5
Has offered us a bribe in the past	1	2	3	4	5
Knowingly over-commits resources or production schedules	1	2	3	4	5

Please answer the following eight questions as they apply to your relationship with the supplier.

	To No Extent	Little Extent	Some Extent	Great Extent	Very Great Extent
I consider my relationship with the supplier rather unpleasant	1	2	3	4	5
I feel fairly satisfied with my relationship with the supplier	1	2	3	4	5
I find real enjoyment in dealing with the supplier	1	2	3	4	5
I am able to purchase reasonably priced products or services from the supplier	1	2	3	4	5
I am able to obtain products or services from the supplier that are of sufficient quality	1	2	3	4	5
I am able to obtain products or services from the supplier with adequate lead times	1	2	3	4	5
The supplier is willing to make adjustments to its schedule to accommodate rush orders	1	2	3	4	5
The supplier does its job properly and efficiently	1	2	3	4	5

The following questions consider certain actions and activities undertaken by your firm that might affect the level of ethical or unethical behavior in dealing with international suppliers. Please circle your answer.

	Never	Seldom	Occasionally	Often	Always
The formal evaluations that I have received take into consideration how ethical my behavior has been	1	2	3	4	5
There are explicit sanctions and punishments in my firm associated with unethical behavior	1	2	3	4	5
Sanctions and punishments against unethical behavior are enforced	1	2	3	4	5
Unethical behavior is rewarded in my company	1	2	3	4	5
The co-workers in my department act in an ethical manner	1	2	3	4	5
My company's own sales force acts in an ethical manner	1	2	3	4	5
My immediate supervisor acts in an ethical manner	1	2	3	4	5
Top purchasing management acts in an ethical manner	1	2	3	4	5
Top company management acts in an ethical manner	1	2	3	4	5
I feel pressure to perform well in my position	1	2	3	4	5

	Strongly Disagree	Disagree	Undecided	Agree	Strongly Agree
I am seeking promotion in my company	1	2	3	4	5
I am seeking a salary increase in my company	1	2	3	4	5
I feel pressure to meet or exceed performance objectives	1	2	3	4	5

Please circle your answer to the following questions

Our company has a corporate code of ethics	Yes	No	
We have a code of ethics dealing with activities specific to purchasing	Yes	No	
I have been required to read our code of ethics	Yes	No	N/A
We periodically communicate our ethical standards to suppliers	Yes	No	N/A
My firm has an ethics committee	Yes	No	
My firm has an ethics hotline	Yes	No	
My firm performs an ethics audit or has some other way of reviewing the actions of the purchasing department to ensure ethical behavior	Yes	No	
Gratuities from *domestic* suppliers are allowed in the amount of:	$_____		

continued from previous page

Gratuities from *international* suppliers are allowed
in the amount of: $_____

	No Training	1-3 Hours	Half Day	One Day	>1 Day
I have received training in ethical issues from my firm	No Training	1-3 Hours	Half Day	One Day	>1 Day
No matter who they are talking with, my co-workers are always good listeners	True	False			
My co-workers do not find it particularly difficult to get along with loud-mouthed, obnoxious people	True	False			
I have never felt the urge to tell someone off at my work	True	False			
My co-workers are always willing to admit when they make a mistake	True	False			

The following questions explore your thoughts concerning your satisfaction with your current position in your firm and your relationship with other departments in your company. Please circle the level to which you *Agree* or *Disagree* with the statements.

	Strongly Disagree	Disagree	Undecided	Agree	Strongly Agree
My job is like a hobby to me	1	2	3	4	5
My job is usually interesting enough to keep me from getting bored	1	2	3	4	5
I consider my job rather unpleasant	1	2	3	4	5
I feel fairly satisfied with my present job	1	2	3	4	5
I find real enjoyment in my work	1	2	3	4	5
People from the various interrelated departments that I interact with make an effort to avoid creating problems or interfering with each other's duties and responsibilities	1	2	3	4	5
People from different departments who have to work with the purchasing function do their jobs properly and efficiently without getting in each other's way	1	2	3	4	5
The work assignments of people from the different departments who work with purchasing are well planned	1	2	3	4	5
The routines of the different departments that have to work with purchasing are well established	1	2	3	4	5

These final questions explore important characteristics of your firm, your supplier's firm, and the type of relationship that exists between your firms.

A *partnership* is defined here as an ongoing relationship with the supplier, involving commitment over an extended period of time, and a mutual sharing of information; it may also include a sharing of risks and rewards of the relationship. A *strategic alliance* is defined here as a relationship with the supplier that has resulted in the formation of a new business operation such as a product development team, a research project, or a manufacturing facility for strategic purposes.

The type of relationship that my firm has with the selected supplier is best characterized as (**please *circle* one**):

< —— >

| Occasional | Repeated | Long-term | | Strategic |
| Transaction | Transactions | Contract | Partnership | Alliance |

In what country is the supplier whom you chose located? _____

What is the primary commodity or material that you purchase from the supplier? _____

What is the approximate volume of purchases from your supplier? $_____

What are the approximate annual sales of your supplier? $_____

How long have you been doing business with the supplier? _____

What is the primary nature of your business? (Examples: manufacturing, service, retail)

_____

What industry are you in? _____

What were the approximate annual sales of your firm during the past fiscal year? $_____

What was the approximate net profit of your firm during the past fiscal year? $_____

What is your title? _____

Have you received the C.P.M. certification from NAPM? Yes:_____ No:_____

Please mail this completed questionnaire in the enclosed envelope to:

Craig R. Carter, Ph.D.
Center For Advanced Purchasing Studies
2055 East Centennial Circle
P.O. Box 22160
Tempe, AZ 85285-2160
Phone: (602) 752-2277, Fax: (602) 491-7885

_____ This number is used *solely* for tracking purposes. Confidentiality of your responses will be *strictly enforced.*

Is there anything else you would like to tell us regarding your involvement in the various ethical activities that have been mentioned? If so, please use this space for that purpose.

Your contribution to this effort is very greatly appreciated. If you would like a summary of the results, please provide the following information or attach a business card.

NAME_____ COMPANY _____

ADDRESS _____

APPENDIX C: A SURVEY OF PURCHASING'S INVOLVEMENT IN INTERNATIONAL SOURCING: SUPPLIER SURVEY •

This survey is being conducted by a researcher for the Center for Advanced Purchasing Studies, and is being sent to you by one of your customers whose name appears at the top of the next page.

Your responses will be used to assess ethical issues in international buyer-supplier relationships. It is extremely important that you answer all questions regarding your firm's activities as **honestly** and **accurately** as possible. Your responses will remain **confidential.**

Please answer **all** questions. If you are not sure of an answer to a question, please provide your **best** estimate. Your contribution to this effort is very greatly appreciated. If you would like a summary of the results, please include a business card with the returned survey.

Thank you for your help.

Craig R. Carter
Center For Advanced Purchasing Studies
2055 East Centennial Circle
P.O. Box 22160
Tempe, AZ 85285-2160
U.S.A.

This survey has been sent by (*name of customer*): _____

This first set of questions explores the activities of *your* firm (not necessarily yourself) in dealing with the U.S. customer/buyer. Please circle your answers.

Currently, our *firm*:	Never	Seldom	Occasionally	Often	Always
Uses less competitive prices or terms for buyers who purchase exclusively from us	1	2	3	4	5
Uses backdoor selling techniques such as approaching personnel in engineering, manufacturing, or other departments outside of purchasing	1	2	3	4	5
Increases prices when there is a shortage of supply of the purchased material or product	1	2	3	4	5
Offers gifts to our customer	1	2	3	4	5
Asks customers for information about our competitors	1	2	3	4	5
Uses obscure contract terms to gain an advantage over customers	1	2	3	4	5
Uses bribery when dealing with customers	1	2	3	4	5
Exaggerates the seriousness of a problem to gain concessions	1	2	3	4	5
Lies or grossly misleads customers in a negotiation	1	2	3	4	5
Has offered customers a bribe in the past	1	2	3	4	5
Knowingly over-commits resources or production schedules	1	2	3	4	5

This next set of questions asks about various activities of the *U.S. customer.* Please circle your answer.

Currently, our *customer:*	Never	Seldom	Occasionally	Often	Always
Allows a supplier to rebid after the closing date	1	2	3	4	5
Allows only certain suppliers to bid	1	2	3	4	5
Gives preference to suppliers preferred by their engineering department	1	2	3	4	5
Allows personalities of our firm to impact decisions	1	2	3	4	5
Writes specifications that favor a particular supplier	1	2	3	4	5
Invents (makes up) a second source of supply to gain competitive advantage over us	1	2	3	4	5
Asks us for information about our competitors	1	2	3	4	5
Uses obscure contract terms to gain an advantage over us	1	2	3	4	5

continued from previous page	Never	Seldom	Occasionally	Often	Always
Exaggerates the seriousness of a problem to gain concessions	1	2	3	4	5
Purposefully misleads us in a negotiation	1	2	3	4	5
Uses bribery when dealing with us	1	2	3	4	5
Overestimates demand to gain volume discounts	1	2	3	4	5
Solicits quotations from suppliers who have little chance of success	1	2	3	4	5
Shows bias against suppliers who use "backdoor" selling	1	2	3	4	5
Cancels purchase orders in progress and tries to avoid cancellation charges	1	2	3	4	5
Allows a supplier to become dependent on the purchasing organization for most of its business	1	2	3	4	5
Uses small payments to facilitate international transactions	1	2	3	4	5

Please answer the following eight questions as they apply to your relationship with the customer.

	To No Extent	Little Extent	Some Extent	Great Extent	Very Great Extent
I consider my relationship with the customer rather unpleasant	1	2	3	4	5
I feel fairly satisfied with my relationship with the customer	1	2	3	4	5
I find real enjoyment in dealing with the customer	1	2	3	4	5
I am able to provide my customer with reasonably priced products or services	1	2	3	4	5
I am able to provide my customer with products or services that are of sufficient quality	1	2	3	4	5
I am able to provide products or services with lead times that are adequate for the customer	1	2	3	4	5
My firm is willing to make adjustments to our schedule to accommodate rush orders for the customer	1	2	3	4	5
We do our job properly and efficiently for the customer	1	2	3	4	5

The following questions consider certain actions and activities undertaken by your firm that might affect the level of ethical or unethical behavior in dealing with U.S. customers.

	Never	Seldom	Occasionally	Often	Always
The formal evaluations that I receive from my supervisor take into consideration how ethical my behavior has been	1	2	3	4	5
There are explicit sanctions and punishments in my firm associated with unethical behavior	1	2	3	4	5
Sanctions and punishments against unethical behavior are enforced	1	2	3	4	5
Unethical behavior is rewarded in my company	1	2	3	4	5
The co-workers in my department act in an ethical manner	1	2	3	4	5
My immediate supervisor acts in an ethical manner	1	2	3	4	5
Top sales or marketing management acts in an ethical manner	1	2	3	4	5
Top company management acts in an ethical manner	1	2	3	4	5
I feel pressure to perform well in my position	1	2	3	4	5

	Strongly Disagree	Disagree	Undecided	Agree	Strongly Agree
I am seeking promotion in my company	1	2	3	4	5
I am seeking a salary increase in my company	1	2	3	4	5
I feel pressure to meet or exceed performance objectives	1	2	3	4	5

Please circle your answer to following questions

Our company has a corporate code of ethics	Yes	No
We have a code of ethics dealing with activities specific to sales	Yes	No
No matter who they are talking with, my co-workers are always good listeners	True	False
My co-workers do not find it particularly difficult to get along with loud-mouthed, obnoxious people	True	False
I have never felt the urge to tell someone off at my work	True	False
My co-workers are always willing to admit when they make a mistake	True	False
Gratuities to *international* customers are allowed in the amount of:	$_____	

These final questions explore important characteristics of your firm, your customer's firm, and the type of relationship which exists between your firms.

A *partnership* is defined here as an ongoing relationship with the customer, involving commitment over an extended period of time, and a mutual sharing of information; it may also include a sharing of risks and rewards of the relationship. A *strategic alliance* is defined here as a relationship with the customer that has resulted in the formation of a new business operation such as a product development team, a research project, or a manufacturing facility for strategic purposes.

The type of relationship that my firm has with the U.S. customer is best characterized as (Please *circle* one):

<———>

| Occasional Transaction | Repeated Transactions | Long-term Contract | Partnership | Strategic Alliance |

What is the primary commodity or material that you sell to the customer? _____

What is the approximate volume of sales to your customer? $_____

What are the approximate annual sales of your company? $_____

How long have you been doing business with the customer? _____

What is the primary nature of your business? (Examples: manufacturing, service, retail)

_____

Please mail this completed questionnaire in the enclosed envelope to:
Craig R. Carter, Ph.D.
Center For Advanced Purchasing Studies
2055 East Centennial Circle
P.O. Box 22160
Tempe, AZ 85285-2160
Phone: (602) 752-2277
Fax: (602) 491-7885

_____ This number is used *solely* for tracking purposes. Confidentiality of your responses will be *strictly enforced*.

Is there anything else you would like to tell us regarding your involvement in the various ethical activities that have been mentioned? If so, please use this space for that purpose.

Also, any comments that you think may help in future efforts to understand the involvement of marketing and sales in these activities will be appreciated.

Your contribution to this effort is very greatly appreciated. If you would like a summary of the results, please provide the following information or attach a business card.

NAME_____ COMPANY _____

ADDRESS _____

APPENDIX D: FACTOR ANALYSES •

ACTIVITIES COMPRISING UNETHICAL BEHAVIOR IN BUYER-SUPPLIER RELATIONSHIPS

The focus group interviews were conducted with purchasing managers from companies that purchase from international suppliers. These firms represented a diverse group of industries, including consumer products, aerospace, pharmaceuticals, construction equipment, and foodstuffs. The literature review identified a wide range of activities that have been included under the general rubric of unethical behavior in buyer-supplier relationships. The interviews with purchasing managers identified many of the same activities, which were listed in Table 1.

Given the large number of activities that might comprise unethical behavior in buyer-supplier relationships, a set of exploratory factor analyses was first conducted to determine whether the scale items that comprised the buyer's as well as the supplier's involvement in these activities were represented by a single dimension, or whether the ethicality of activities of each party were represented by more than one dimension. After conducting the exploratory factor analysis, confirmatory factor analyses were conducted to further assess the unidimensionality, reliability, and validity of the resulting scales. Confirmatory factor analyses were also used to assess the scale items representing the antecedents to (such as pressure to perform and actions of co-workers) and consequences of (e.g., effectiveness of the buyer-supplier relationship) unethical practices in buyer-supplier relationships.

Unethical Activities: Buyer

The items listed in Table 1 that were specifically applicable to the purchasing organization appear in Table 10. These items were subjected to an exploratory factor analysis (EFA). Factors were extracted using the principal factor method, followed by a varimax (orthogonal) rotation. Both the eigenvalue-one and scree test (Catell, 1966) criteria suggested the presence of two meaningful factors, which were retained for the rotation. The corresponding factor loadings are also presented in Table 10.

TABLE 10
SURVEY ITEMS AND CORRESPONDING FACTOR PATTERN: BUYER ACTIVITIES

Factor Pattern 1	2	Survey	Item
0.06	0.54	1.	Allows a supplier to rebid after the closing date
0.08	0.40	2.	Allows only certain suppliers to bid
0.04	0.64	3.	Gives preference to suppliers preferred by top management
0.05	0.71	4.	Allows the personalities of the supplier to impact decisions
0.24	0.65	5.	Writes specifications that favor a particular supplier
0.59	0.03	6.	Invents (makes up) a second source of supply to gain competitive advantage
0.21	0.18	7.	Asks suppliers for information about our competitors
0.70	0.07	8.	Uses obscure contract terms to gain advantage over suppliers
0.77	0.07	9.	Exaggerates the seriousness of a problem to gain concessions
0.69	0.01	10.	Purposefully misleads a salesperson in a negotiation
0.22	0.26	11.	Uses bribery when dealing in foreign markets
0.43	0.29	12.	Overestimates demand to gain volume discounts
0.53	0.40	13.	Solicits quotations from suppliers who have little chance of success
0.48	0.14	14.	Shows bias against suppliers who use "backdoor" selling techniques such as approaching personnel in engineering, manufacturing, or other departments outside of purchasing
0.40	0.22	15.	Cancels purchase orders in progress and tries to avoid cancellation charges
0.31	0.33	16.	Allows a supplier to become dependent on the purchasing organization for most of its business
0.18	0.35	17.	Uses small payments to facilitate international transactions

An item was considered to load on a given factor if the factor loading from the rotated factor pattern was 0.40 or greater for that factor, and was less than 0.40 for the other. Based on these criteria, seven items were found to load on the first factor. Of these seven items, four items were found to load very highly on the first factor (items 6, 8, 9, and 10), with almost no loading on the second factor. The items that loaded highly on the first factor included such activities as using obscure contract terms to gain advantage over the supplier and purposefully misleading the supplier. The first factor seemed to consist of activities involving deception, and was subsequently labeled *deceitful practices*.

Five items loaded on the second factor (items 1, 2, 3, 4, and 5). Here, the items included somewhat more subtle activities such as allowing suppliers to rebid after the closing date and giving preference to suppliers preferred by top management. The second factor was subsequently labeled *subtle practices*.

While EFA is a useful preliminary technique for scale construction, "undimensionality cannot be assessed unless a subsequent confirmatory factor analysis (CFA) is used to evaluate and likely refine the resulting scales" (Gerbing & Anderson, 1988, pp. 189). The two dimensions of unethical buyer practices were next subjected to a CFA, using the CALIS procedure in SAS. The advantages of using the CALIS procedure rather than the more commonly used FACTOR procedure is that the CALIS procedure provides both a chi-square test for the null hypothesis that the theoretical model fits the data and a number of descriptive goodness of fit statistics (Ahire, Golhar, & Waller, 1996).

Researchers using confirmatory factor analysis in the CALIS procedure in SAS use a chi-square test to determine whether the hypothesized model fits the data. One problem with examining only the chi-square test is that with real-world data, the chi-square statistic will frequently be significant even if the model provides a good fit (James, Mulaik, & Brett, 1982). For this reason, researchers generally supplement the chi-square test with a number of other stand-alone goodness-of-fit indices.

One commonly used fit index is the goodness-of-fit index (GFI). Values on this index range from 0 to 1, with values over 0.9 generally indicative of an acceptable fit of the model to the data (Bollen, 1989). Other indices include Bentler and Bonett's (1980) non-normed fit index (NNFI) and Bentler's (1989) comparative fit index (CFI) as overall goodness-of-fit indices. These indices are often preferable to other commonly used indices such as the GFI, as they are less likely to produce biased estimates in small samples (Marsh, Balla, & McDonald, 1988; Bentler, 1989). Like the GFI, values over 0.9 on the NNFI and CFI indicate an acceptable fit. In addition to high values on these fit indices, significant factor loadings of the scale items are also desirable. Finally, Anderson and Gerbing note that "the patterning of the residuals has been the most useful for locating the source

of misspecification in multiple-indicator measurement models" (Anderson & Gerbing 1988, pp. 417). Items that resulted in significant standardized residuals were examined as possible candidates for elimination, for reasons including the fact that the items may have been considered by the respondents to be highly similar.

The survey questions at the top of Table 11 (deceitful practices and subtle practices) resulted in a two factor model that displayed a non-significant chi-square value (p=0.40) and resulted in values of 0.95, 1.00, and 1.00 for the GFI, CFI, and NNFI, respectively. These findings suggest an excellent fit of the data to the measurement model. In addition, there were no large normalized residuals, all factor loadings were significant, and the reliability coefficients were above the 0.60 minimum recommended by Nunnally (1978) for exploratory research. These goodness-of-fit indices and reliability values are shown separately in Table 12.

Due to the small sample size, the CFA was conducted on the same sample of buyers as was the exploratory factor analysis. The use of the same sample for both analyses can result in the capitalization of chance since the data sets were identical. As a result, a second CFA was conducted using the suppliers' answers to the same survey questions displayed in Table 11. A similar pattern of factor loadings was found for this second CFA, with an insignificant x^2 value (p=0.7265), and GFI, CFI, and NNFI indices of 0.95, 1.00, and 1.00 respectively. The findings from this second CFA suggest that activities that were identified as unethical by American buyers were viewed in a similar fashion by their international suppliers.

Unethical Activities: Supplier

The items displayed in Table 1 that were specifically applicable to supplier actions were also subjected to an exploratory factor analysis. Factors were extracted using the principal factor method, followed by a varimax (orthogonal) rotation. Both the eigenvalue-one and scree test (Catell 1966) criteria suggested the presence of a single meaningful factor. This single-factor solution was subjected to a CFA, using the CALIS procedure in SAS. After the elimination of scale items that resulted in high normalized residuals, the revised model displayed a non-significant chi-square value (p=0.24) and resulted in values of 0.96, 0.98, and 0.98 for the GFI, CFI, and NNFI, respectively. These findings suggest an excellent fit of the data to the measurement model. In addition, there were no large normalized residuals, and all factor loadings were significant. The scale items with their associated factor loadings are also presented in Table 11.

Again, due to the small sample size of buyers, a second confirmatory factor analysis was conducted on the supplier sample. A similar pattern of factor loadings was found for this second CFA, with an insignificant x^2 value (p=0.22), and GFI, CFI, and NNFI indices of 0.94, 0.94, and 0.92 respectively.

TABLE 11
QUESTIONNAIRE SCALE ITEMS [a]

Buyer Activities: Deceitful Practices
Currently, our purchasing function [b]
- Invents (makes up) a second source of supply to gain competitive advantage (.56)
- Uses obscure contract terms to gain an advantage over suppliers (.64)
- Exaggerates the seriousness of a problem to gain concessions (.71)
- Purposefully misleads a salesperson in a negotiation (.62)

Buyer Activities: Subtle Practices
Currently, our purchasing function
- Gives preference to suppliers preferred by top management (.45)
- Allows personalities of the supplier to impact decisions (.54)
- Writes specifications that favor a particular supplier (.77)

Supplier Activities
Currently, the supplier [b]
- Uses less competitive prices or terms for buyers who purchase exclusively from the supplier (.52)
- Uses backdoor selling techniques (such as approaching personnel in engineering, manufacturing, or other departments outside of purchasing) (.75)
- Increases prices when there is a shortage of supply of the purchased material or product (.52)
- Offers gifts in excess of nominal value (.58)
- Asks us for information about their competitors (.47)
- Uses obscure contract terms to gain an advantage over us (.65)
- Lies to or grossly misleads us in a negotiation (.63)
- Knowingly over-commits resources or production schedules (.62)

Leadership [b]
- My immediate supervisor acts in an ethical manner (.92)
- Top purchasing management acts in an ethical manner (.96)
- Top company management acts in an ethical manner (.84)

Actions of Co-workers [b]
- The co-workers in my department act in an ethical manner (.87)
- My company's own sales force acts in an ethical manner (.66)

Evaluation and Sanctions [b]
- The formal evaluations that I have received take into consideration how ethical my behavior has been (.52)
- There are explicit sanctions and punishments in my firm associated with unethical behavior (.79)
- Sanctions and punishments against unethical behavior are enforced (.78)

Training [c]
- I have received training in ethical issues from my firm

Pressure to Perform [d]
- I feel pressure to perform well in my position (.71)
- I feel pressure to meet or exceed performance expectations (.94)

Supplier Relationship [e]
- The type of relationship that my firm has with the selected supplier is best characterized as

Length of Relationship
- How long have you been doing business with the supplier?

National Culture
- In what country is the supplier whom you chose located?

Effectiveness of Buyer-Supplier Relationship [f]
- I am able to purchase reasonably priced products or services from the supplier (.69)
- I am able to obtain products or services from the supplier that are of sufficient quality (.75)
- I am able to obtain products or services from the supplier with adequate lead times (.69)
- The supplier does its job properly and efficiently (.71)

Satisfaction with Buyer-Supplier Relationship [f]
- I consider my relationship with the supplier rather unpleasant (.70) [g]
- I feel fairly satisfied with my relationship with the supplier (.92)

[a] Standardized factor loadings in parentheses.
[b] These items were measured on a 5 point Likert scale where 1 = Never and 5 = Always.
[c] This item was measured on a 5 point Likert scale, where 1 = No training and 5 = More Than One Day.
[d] These items were measured on a 5 point Likert scale where 1 = Strongly Disagree and 5 = Strongly Agree.
[e] This item was measured on a 5 point Likert scale, where 1 = Occasional Transaction, 3 = Long-Term Contract, and 5 = Joint Venture.
[f] These items were measured on a 5 point Likert scale where 1 = To No Extent and 5 = To A Very Great Extent.
[g] These items were reverse coded.

TABLE 12
DESCRIPTIVE STATISTICS OF THE MODEL CONSTRUCTS

Construct	Reliability [a]	GFI [b]	χ^2/df [c]	CFI [b]	NNFI [b]
Buyer Activities: Deceitful Practices	0.70	0.96	22.4/24 (p=.55)	1.00	1.00
Buyer Activities: Subtle Practices	0.61	0.96	22.4/24 (p=.55)	1.00	1.00
Supplier Activities	0.79	0.96	24.1/20 (p=.24)	0.98	0.98
Leadership	0.93	0.99	3.1/4 (p=.55)	1.00	1.00
Actions of Co-workers	0.73	0.99	1.5/1 (p=.22)	1.00	0.98
Evaluation and Sanctions	0.69	0.99	4.8/4 (p=.31)	1.00	0.99
Training	—-	—-	—-	—-	—-
Pressure to Perform	0.80	0.99	3.1/4 (p=.55)	1.00	1.00
Supplier Relationship	—-	—-	—-	—-	—-
National Culture	—-	—-	—-	—-	—-
Effectiveness of Buyer-Supplier Relationship	0.80	0.96	18.8/13 (p=.13)	0.98	0.97
Satisfaction with Buyer-Supplier Relationship	0.78	0.99	4.8/4 (p=.31)	1.00	0.99

[a] Reliability values greater than .60 indicate acceptable reliability for exploratory research.
[b] Values of .90 and higher on the GFI, CFI, and NNFI indicate an acceptable fit of the measurement model to the data.
[c] Insignificant χ^2 values indicate an acceptable fit of the measurement model to the data.

OTHER SCALES: ANTECEDENTS AND CONSEQUENCES

Confirmatory factor analyses were conducted for all the multi-item scales used to measure the antecedents and consequences of unethical activities shown in Figure 1. The scale items that were retained to measure these constructs are displayed in Table 11, and the fit indices and reliability values are shown in Table 12. All the remaining scale items displayed insignificant χ^2 values with GFI, CFI, and NNFI values all far in excess of the 0.90 minimums. In addition, all scale items had significant factor loadings (p<0.0001). Together, these values suggest that the scales were unidimensional (Gerbing and Anderson 1988) and display convergent validity (Anderson and Gerbing 1988). In addition, all scales had Cronbach coefficient alpha values in excess of the 0.60 recommended minimum (Nunnally 1978; Cronbach, 1951).

Single-Item Measures

Finally, note that the fit indices and reliability values were not shown for some constructs, such as the type of buyer-supplier relationship and national culture. These constructs were measured with a single survey question, due to both constraints associated with the survey length as well as the fact that it was appropriate to measure some constructs with only a single question. For example, a single item indicator was appropriate for assessing the country were the supplier was located. The country of the supplier was used as a proxy for national culture, which is the same proxy measurement used by Hofstede (1980). The length of the buyer-supplier relationship was measured in years, so a single-item was appropriate here as well (Bucklin & Sengupta, 1993).

While the type of supplier relationship was assessed using a single question, the various response options were clearly defined. For example, in distinguishing between a partnership and a strategic alliance, a partnership was defined as "an ongoing relationship with the supplier, involving commitment over an extended period of time, and a mutual sharing of information; it may also include a sharing of risks and rewards of the relationship." A strategic alliance was defined as "a relationship with the supplier that has resulted in the formation of a new business operation such as a product development team, a research project, or a manufacturing facility for strategic purposes."

APPENDIX E: REFERENCES •

Ahire, S.L., Golhar, D.Y., & Waller, M.A. (1996). Development and validation of TQM implementation constructs. *Decision Sciences,* 27 (1), 23-56.

Anderson, J.C. & Gerbing, D.W. (1988). Structural equation modeling in practice: A review and recommended two-step approach. *Psychological Bulletin,* 103(3), 411-423.

Armacost, R.L., Hosseini, J.C., Morris, S.A., & Rehbein, K.A. (1991). An empirical comparison of direct questioning, scenario, and randomized response methods for obtaining sensitive business information. *Decision Sciences,* 22(5), 1073-1090.

Armstrong, J.S. & Overton, T.S. (1977). Estimating non-response bias in mail surveys. *Journal of Marketing Research,* 14(3), 396-402.

Becker, H. & Fritzsche, D.J. (1987). A comparison of ethical behavior of American, French, and German managers. *Columbia Journal of World Business,* 22(4), 87-95.

Beets, S.D. & Killough, L.N. (1990). The effectiveness of a complaint-based ethics enforcement system: Evidence from the accounting profession. *Journal of Business Ethics,* 9, 115-126.

Berry, B. (1995). A higher standard. *Iron Age New Steel,* 11(9), 2.

Bentler, P.M. (1989). *EQS structural equations program manual.* Los Angeles: BMDP Statistical Software.

Bentler, P.M. & Bonett, D.G. (1980). Significance tests and goodness-of-fit in the analysis of covariance structures. *Psychological Bulletin,* 88(3), 588-606.

Bollen, K.A. (1989). *Structural equations with latent variables.* New York: Wiley.

Bucklin, L.P. & Sengupta, S. (1993). "Organizing successful co-marketing alliances," *Journal of Marketing,* 57(2), 32-46.

Calder, B.J. (1977). Focus groups and the nature of qualitative marketing research. *Journal of Marketing Research,* 14(August), 353-364.

Cattell, R.B. (1966). The scree test for the number of factors. *Multivariate Behavior Research,* 1(2), 245-276.

Chonko, L.B. & Hunt, S.D. (1985). Ethics and marketing management: An empirical investigation. *Journal of Business Research,* 13(4), 339-359.

Chonko, L.B., Tanner, Jr., J.F., & Weeks, W.A. (1996). Ethics in salesperson decision making: A synthesis of research approaches and an extension of the scenario method. *Journal of Personal Selling and Sales Management,* 16(1), 35-52.

Churchill, G.A., Ford, N.M., Hartley, S.W., & Walker, Jr., O.C. (1985). The determinants of salesperson performance: A meta-analysis," *Journal of Marketing Research,* 22(2), 103-118.

Cronbach, L.J. (1951). Coefficient Alpha and the internal structure of tests. *Psychometricka,* 16(3): 297-334.

Crowne, D.P. & Marlowe, D. (1960). A new scale of social desirability independent of psychopathology. *Journal of Consulting Psychology,* 24(4), 349-354.

Dobler, D.W. & Burt, D.N. (1996). *Purchasing and Supply Management.* New York: McGraw-Hill Inc.

Donaldson, T. (1996). Values in tension. *Harvard Business Review,* 74(5), 48-62.

Dubinsky, A.J. & Gwin, J.M. (1981). Business ethics: buyers and sellers. *Journal of Purchasing and Materials Management,* 17(4), 9-16.

Ellram, L.M. & Cooper, M.C. (1990). Supply chain management, partnerships, and the shipper-third party relationship. *International Journal of Logistics Management,* 1(2), 1-10.

Ellram, L.M. (1991). Supply chain management, the industrial organisation perspective. *International Journal of Physical Distribution and Logistics Management,* 21(1), 13-22.

England, G.W. (1975). *The manager and his values: An international perspective.* Cambridge: Ballinger Publishing Company.

Epstein, E.M. (1989). Business ethics, corporate good citizenship, and the corporate social policy press: A view from the United States. *Journal of Business Ethics,* 8(8), 583-595.

Felch, R.I. (1985). Standards of conduct: The key to supplier relations. *Journal of Purchasing and Materials Management,* 21(3), 16-18.

Ferrell, O.C. & Gresham, L.G. (1985). A contingency framework for understanding ethical decision making in marketing. *Journal of Marketing,* 49(3), 87-96.

Forker, L.B. & Janson, R.L. (1990). Ethical practices in purchasing. *Journal of Purchasing and Materials Management,* 26(1), 19-26.

Frazier, G.L., Spekman, R.E., & O'Neal, C.R. (1988). Just-in-time exchange relationships in industrial markets. *Journal of Marketing,* 52(4), 52-67.

Frederick, W.C. (1991). The moral authority of transnational corporate codes. *Journal of Business Ethics,* 10(3), 165-177.

Fritzsche, D.J. & Becker, H. (1983). Ethical behavior of marketing managers. *Journal of Business Ethics,* 2, 291-299.

Gardner, J. & Cooper, M.C. (1988). *Elements of strategic partnership. in Partnerships: A natural evolution in logistics.* J.E. McKeon ed., Cleveland: Logistics Resource, Inc., 15-32.

Gatewood, R.D. & Carroll, A.B. (1991). Assessment of ethical performance of organization members: A conceptual framework. *Academy of Management Review,* 16(4), 667-690.

Gerbing, D.W. & Anderson, J.C. (1988). An updated paradigm for scale development incorporating unidimensionality and its assessment. *Journal of Marketing Research,* 25(2), 186-192.

Hendrick, T.E. & Ellram, L.M. (1993). *Strategic supplier partnerships: An international study.* Tempe, AZ: Center For Advanced Purchasing Studies.

Hofstede, G. (1980). *Culture's Consequences.* Beverly Hills, CA: Sage.

Houlihan, J.B. (1985). International supply chain management. International *Journal of Physical Distribution and Materials Management,* 15(1), 22-38.

Hunt, S.D., Chonko, L.B., & Wilcox, J.B. (1984). Ethical problems of marketing researchers. *Journal of Marketing Research,* 21(3), 309-324.

Hunt, S.D. & Vitell, S.J. (1986). A general theory of marketing ethics. *Journal of Macromarketing,* 6(1), 5-16.

Husted, B.W., Dozier, J.B., McMahon, J.T., & Kattan, M.W. (1996). The impact of cross-national carriers of business ethics on attitudes about questionable practices and form of moral reasoning. *Journal of International Business Studies,* 27(2), 391-411.

James, L.R., Mulaik, S.A., & Brett, J.M. (1982). *Causal analysis.* Beverly Hills, CA: Sage.

Janson, R.L. (1988). *Purchasing Ethical Practices.* Tempe, AZ: Center For Advanced Purchasing Studies.

Krueger, R. (1988). *Focus Groups.* Newbury Park, CA: Sage.

Lambert, D.M. & Harrington, T.C. (1990). Measuring nonresponse bias in customer service mail surveys. *Journal of Business Logistics,* 11(2), 5-25.

Leenders, M.R. & Fearon, H.E. (1993). *Purchasing and materials management.* Tenth Edition. Homewood: Richard D. Irwin, Inc.

Levy, M. & Dubinsky, A.J. (1983). Identifying and addressing retail salespeople's ethical problems: A method and application. *Journal of Retailing,* 59(1), 46-66.

Marsh, H.W., Balla, J.R., & McDonald, R.P. (1988). Goodness-of-fit indexes in confirmatory factor analysis: The effect of sample size. *Psychological Bulletin,* 103, 391-410.

Mathews, M.C. (1987). Codes of ethics: Organizational behavior and misbehavior. *Research in Corporate Social Performance and Policy,* 9, 107-130.

McQuarrie, E.F. and McIntyre, S.H. (1988). Conceptual underpinnings for the use of group interviews in consumer research. *Advances in Consumer Research,* 15, 580-586.

Mitchell, T.R., Daniels, D., Hopper, H., George-Falvy, J., & Ferris, G.R. (1996). Perceived correlates of illegal behavior in organizations. *Journal of Business Ethics,* 15(4), 429-455.

Murphy, P.E. (1989). Creating ethical corporate structures. *Sloan Management Review,* 30(2), 81-87.

Neter, J., Wasserman, W., & Kutner, M.H. (1990). *Applied Linear Statistical Models.* New York: Irwin.

Nunnally, J. (1978). *Psychometric theory.* New York: McGraw-Hill.

Osborn, R.N. & Hunt, J.C. (1974). Environment and organizational effectiveness. *Administrative Science Quarterly,* 19(June), 231-46.

Pitman, G.A. & Sanford, J.P. (1994). The Foreign Corrupt Practices Act revisited: Attempting to regulate ethical bribes in global business. *International Journal of Purchasing and Materials Management,* 30(3), 15-20.

Puffer, S.M. & McCarthy, D.J. (1995). Finding the common ground in Russian and American business ethics. *California Management Review,* 37(2), 29-46.

Robin, D.P. & Reidenbach, R.E. (1987). Social responsibility, ethics, and marketing strategy: Closing the gap between concept and application. *Journal of Marketing,* 51(January), 44-58.

Rowan, R.L. & Campbell, D.C. (1983). The attempt to regulate industrial relations through international codes of conduct." *Columbia Journal of World Business,* 18(2), 64-72.

Rudelius, W. & Buchholz, R.A. (1979). What industrial purchasers see as key ethical dilemmas. *Journal of Purchasing and Materials Management,* 15(4), 2-10.

Schlegelmilch, B.B. & Robertson, D.C. (1995). The influence of country and industry on ethical perceptions of senior executives in the U.S. and Europe. *Journal of International Business Studies,* 26(4), 859-881.

Trevino, L.K. (1992). Ethical decision making in organizations: A person-situation interactionist model. *Academy of Management Review,* 11(3), 601-617.

Trevisan, R.E. (1986). Developing a statement of ethics: A case study. *Journal of Purchasing and Materials Management,* 22(3), 8-14.

Turner, G.B., Taylor, G.S., & Hartley, M.F. (1994). Ethics policies and gratuity acceptance by purchasers. *International Journal of Purchasing and Materials Management,* 30(3), 43-47.

van den Hengel, J. (1995). Purchasing ethics: Strain or strategy? *Purchasing and Supply Management,* September, 50-52.

Webster, F.J. (1992). The changing role of marketing in the corporation. *Journal of Marketing,* 56(4), 1-17.

Weitz, B.A. (1981). Effectiveness in sales interactions: A contingency framework. *Journal of Marketing,* 45(1), 85-103.

Williams, A.J., Guinipero, L.C., & Henthorne, T.L. (1994). The cross-functional imperative: the case of marketing and purchasing. *International Journal of Purchasing and Materials Management,* 30(3), 29-33.

Wood, D.J. (1991). Corporate social performance revisited. *Academy of Management Review,* 16(4), 691-718.

CENTER FOR ADVANCED PURCHASING STUDIES •

THE CENTER FOR ADVANCED PURCHASING STUDIES (CAPS) was established in November 1986 as the result of an affiliation agreement between the College of Business at Arizona State University and the National Association of Purchasing Management. It is located at The Arizona State University Research Park, 2055 East Centennial Circle, P.O. Box 22160, Tempe, Arizona 85285-2160 (Telephone [602] 752-2277).

The Center has three major goals to be accomplished through its research program:

to improve purchasing effectiveness and efficiency;
to improve overall purchasing capability;
to increase the competitiveness of U.S. companies in a global economy.

Research published includes 32 focus studies on purchasing/materials management topics ranging from purchasing organizational relationships to CEOs' expectations of the purchasing function, as well as benchmarking reports on purchasing performance in 26 industries.

Research under way includes: *The Impact of Purchasing on Financial Performance; Developing Internet Electronic Commerce Strategies for Purchasing and Supply Chain Management; Corporate Implementation Strategies for ISO 14000;* and the benchmarking reports of purchasing performance by industry.

CAPS, affiliated with two 501 (c) (3) educational organizations, is funded solely by tax-deductible contributions from organizations and individuals who want to make a difference in the state of purchasing and materials management knowledge. Policy guidance is provided by the Board of Trustees consisting of: